PRAISE FOR BRIAN RUHE and *FREEING THE BUDDHA*

As a university instructor, I know how difficult it sometimes is to teach adults, who often hold entrenched preconceived notions and resist direction. Brian's absolute openness and respect for his students is entirely disarming; he takes every question, comment, and challenge seriously, using them to present fresh information and insight into the tenets of Buddhism. His lectures are filled with self-deprecating humour, amusing anecdotes, and everyday examples, making accessible what could be rather heavy material. At the same time, I never doubted the sincerity of his spirituality, which comes across without any tinge of New Age hucksterism. He has a deep life commitment to spreading the Buddha's message. In other words, he is the perfect instructor for both neophytes and experienced practitioners. *Karen Ferguson, Ph.D. Simon Fraser University, Department of History*

BUDDHISM IN CANADA
Edited by Bruce Matthews
The Theravada Buddhist Community of Vancouver is a network of local sitting groups and sponsored classes in Buddhism and vipassana ('inward vision', 'insight meditation'), brought together by the efforts of Brian Ruhe, a Theravada enthusiast.

SHARED VISION MAGAZINE
Review by Publisher Rex Weyler
Brian Ruhe starts where all good Buddhists start, with silence and the breath. *Freeing the Buddha* reviews why and how Buddhists meditate, and why paying attention to our breath and to the inner thought process leads to awareness and right action. The book makes it clear why Buddhism is distinct from the world's other main religions, based on the knowledge of mental states that can only be discovered through personal introspection. Ruhe provides excellent expositions on abstruse Buddhist concepts. No single book could ever completely cover the vast subject of Buddhism, but *Freeing the Buddha* is a respectable start and a valuable resource.

BC BOOKWORLD
Alan Twigg, Publisher

"All Star Universal Wrestling is a teacher," says Brian Ruhe, who teaches Buddhism at Douglas College. Ruhe's book offers 'a dangerous collection of essays' meant to incite, not unlike WWF theatrical performers.

MIDWEST BOOK REVIEW (U.S.)
James A. Cox - Editor-in-Chief

This course on major aspects of Buddhism adds controversial essays which challenge conventional teachings on Buddhism, providing not only an overview of Buddhist belief systems and teachings, but their applications throughout history. The author, a Buddhist teacher and prior monk, provides a very different perspective on Buddhist beliefs and their applications, adding a welcome dose of humor along with many insights.

Brian Ruhe taught meditation at some of our branches and his workshops were a great experience for our staff as many discovered meditation for the first time. Brian was clear and easy to understand and his sense of humour made it fun.
Naslishah Alizada Thony, VanCity, Employee Well-Being Specialist

Brian's superb communication skills at the International Buddhist Society, Buddhist temple in Richmond were very helpful in making us understand contemporary Mahayana Buddhist beliefs and practices.
Professor Jurgen Schönwetter, Columbia Bible College, Clearbrook, B.C.

Brian's discourse on Awakened Heart was an inspiration and many were touched by his guided meditation on compassion. It was during the question and answer period that Brian's spontaneity and humour shone the brightest! Everyone felt involved in the seminar and we appreciated his ability to draw out our own wisdom. I highly recommend Brian for other groups who want to hear an uplifting message.
Orai Fujikawa, Resident Minister (Japanese temple),
Vancouver Buddhist Church

A Short Walk On An Ancient Path

A Buddhist Exploration of Meditation, Karma and Rebirth

by Brian Ruhe

Chapters 1, 3, 7 and 8 have been rewritten from *Freeing the Buddha,*
published in 1999, then revised and published by
Motilal Banarsidass Publishers in Delhi, India, in 2005.

ISBN 978-0-9683951-2-7
PRINTED IN CANADA

Published by the Buddhist Spectrum Study Group
www.theravada.ca

Cataloging-in-Publication Data
Ruhe, Brian Anthony, 1959-
A Short Walk On An Ancient Path
Includes bibliographical references and glossary.

Printed by Hignell Book Printing
Winnipeg, Canada

Cover art by Sadra Saffari
Back cover photo by Samsam Juliano

Nakhon Pathom – Phra pathon Chedi, Thailand

Table of Contents

Entrance, Grand Palace, Bangkok

List of Photographs and Illustrations

A Short Walk On An Ancient Path

Acknowledgments

My first book *Freeing the Buddha* was published in paperback in 1999. Since then a revised version was published in hardcover by Motilal Banarsidass Publishers in Delhi, India, in 2005. It was 477 pages long and almost two inches thick. It seems, however, that most people prefer to have a small paperback. I resolved to cut the book in half omitting the more controversial parts.

Chapters 1, 3, 7 and 8 have been rewritten from *Freeing the Buddha* but in the end I have written this almost completely new book which reflects an additional ten years of experience. My students will find that it complements the courses I teach.

I would like to acknowledge Ajahn Sona who has had the biggest influence upon me in the past nine years. I identify with the Theravada Forest tradition that he represents. He has graciously given me permission to include his kamma teachings and his breath and loving kindness meditation instructions in this book.

Special thanks to Venerable Bhikkhu Bodhi for choosing the rebirth essay for this book and giving me permission to quote him extensively, to Ajahn Kusalo for permission to reprint his walking meditation instructions and to Venerable Pavaro for editing the recorded teachings of Ajahn Sona. I appreciate the help of Ajahn Sona's mother, Irma West, who read the manuscript and gave great advice. Barry Millar once again did the layout design and prepress. I thank him and also Sadra Saffari who designed the cover. I appreciate many others who helped and offered suggestions and ideas.

The author as Buddhasaro bhikkhu in 1996

Chapter 1

Four Noble Truths

*"No one and nothing can free you
but your own understanding."*
Ajahn Chah

What did the Buddha say to the hot dog vendor? He said, "Make me one with everything." Then, the vendor gave the Buddha a hot dog with everything on it, mustard, onions and relish. The Buddha gave him a 20 dollar bill, although monks aren't supposed to handle cash. The Buddha waited for his change but the vendor didn't give the Buddha his change. Finally, the Buddha said softly, "Sir, aren't you going to give me my change?" Then the vendor said, "The change must come from within!" So he outsmarted the Buddha himself.

In the Buddha's style of teaching he had little time for rites and rituals. He was a practical teacher, concerned with explaining the nature of suffering and the path to the end of suffering. Unlike most religions, there is no blind faith in Buddhism. You do need to believe in the Buddha's world view of karma and rebirth in order to be a Buddhist. Those are the only two things that you have to believe in order to be a Buddhist, but this is not blind faith. It is saddha, which is the Pali word meaning 'reasoned conviction'. You believe it as a working hypothesis about how to live even though you don't know from your own direct experience if it is true. The Buddha said 'come and see', he didn't say 'come and believe.' The amount of freedom that the Buddha gave to his followers is astonishing to a student of comparative religion. The Buddha didn't want to have tight control over his monks and nuns. He wanted them to be free to work out the truth. His teaching, called dhamma or dharma, is a guide to point you in that direction.

The 'pointing out' instructions in the Buddhist scriptures are not like 'the word of God' in the Bible. The Bible is interpreted by many as the literal word of God so it is very important to theistic people to interpret what it is that God was directing us to do many centuries ago. In Buddhism, the dharma is viewed as pointing out instructions to guide you to working with your mind; to being a decent person, and attaining the direct experience of insight into the nature of things. The Buddha said "The finger points at the moon. Why look at the finger? Look at the moon." This means that the Buddha and the dharma are like a finger pointing at the moon, which is nirvana, enlightened mind. You should follow the finger and reach the goal of seeing the moon, attaining nirvana. Don't get stuck on the person of Gotama Buddha or Jesus Christ. Don't get ensnared debating about the words in the dharma or the Bible. In the Middle East we have Muslims and Jews and Christians fighting each other over the interpretation of the Bible. Buddhism has no history of any religious wars in the past 2500 years.

Interpret the dharma, use the dharma, and apply it to your life situation. It will work to help you to live in the world and to be a saner person. And what people need to be taught is how to live in the world. This dharma has been tested and proven to work for about 2500 years. We don't know exactly when the Buddha lived but it was in the 5th century BC. What matters is how the Buddhist teachings speak to your life now. What can Buddhism do for you and the ones you care about? The historical details of the Buddha's life, what he did and the people around him, are secondary to the importance of how the timeless dhamma can bring strength and guidance to your life. Christmas Humphries, in one of his better moments back in the 1950s, remarked that even if it was discovered that Gotama Buddha did not even exist (he did), Buddhism would still work and it would hardly be affected.

The historical details of Christ's life and particularly his crucifixion are very important and have tremendous meaning. It is absolutely necessary to the Christian religion that Christ's crucifixion did happen and that its meaning was about the atonement of the sins of man. These historical events and others in the Bible, like the book of Genesis, are a big deal. So it is upsetting to some Christians that in recent years New Testament scholars have put forward various ideas about the historical Jesus which contradict some vital concepts in the Bible. One such postulation is that Christ's crucifixion may have occurred by sheer happenstance, called 'the car accident' analogy about Christ's death. There is no such parallel in Buddhism. Regardless of what personal problems Thomas Edison had, we still benefit from the light bulb. today. Buddhism is a different religion than the Bible. Others will say that the Christians and the Buddhists are saying the same thing, but in different ways. It's not true. They are different world views, different paths, going to a different goal. Genuine religious tolerance means accepting and respecting those differences. Trying to convince yourself and others that they are all the same is a form of intolerance.

The fundamental difference in how Buddhists and Christians regard their own scriptures is that Buddhists apply the dharma to work out the truth for themselves and have a direct experience of life and reality without delusions. Christians believe that the Bible is the truth from God and that it must be obeyed.

When I was living in Bangkok I would sit in a smoggy bus for an hour to visit The Dhamma House where my friend Ajhan Helen Jandamit lived and taught courses on Buddhism. She is from England and has taught Vipassana meditation for 20 years in Thailand. She told me that when she was a girl in England she was a sincere Christian and she was taught to love others and have compassion for them. "I tried," she said. "I really tried but they didn't teach me how. I discovered Buddhism when some Thai monks came to England. When I studied

Buddhism I discovered the methods about how to develop loving kindness and how to work with the frustrations and anger that arose in my mind."

Buddhism is very much a 'how to' approach to religion, a do it to yourself project. The emphasis is that here and now is the only time there is and if you don't 'get it' now then you won't automatically 'get it' later when you are dead. Some religions emphasize happiness in the next life, but don't worry about happiness in this life. Other religions say you should be happy in this life, but don't worry about a future life. Buddhism teaches that there shouldn't be any problem between these two. You should be happy in this life and that should lead to happiness in your next life. In the Bible, the emphasis is on a later time, at death. At death you will be rewarded for your patience to go to church on Sundays, and you will get to go to heaven if you've been good. Buddhists are taught to be like the Buddha, to imitate the Buddha, and eventually become an arahant, as the Buddha was. Christians are not taught to be Jesus Christ, and they are not taught to realize their own godhood.

In learning theory it is taught that a teacher must activate prior knowledge. Since this book is published in the West, it is logical to compare Buddhism to the Christian religion as a frame of reference. The purpose is to better understand and illuminate the Buddhist path. Unlike the Bible, the Buddha allowed an incomparable freedom of thought within the sangha. This is because nirvana is dependent upon one's direct realization of the truth, not upon agreeing with the truth or receiving a reward from a god. In the famous Kalama sutta, the Buddha was visiting a small community named Kesaputta in the kingdom of Kosala. The people, the Kalamas, told the Buddha (Colombo, 1929; 115):

> Sir, there are some recluses and brahmanas who visit Kesaputta.
> They explain and illumine only their own doctrines, and despise,
> condemn and spurn others' doctrines. Then come other recluses

and brahmanas, and they too, in their turn, explain and illumine only their own doctrines, and despise, condemn and spurn others' doctrines. But for us Sir, we have always had doubt and perplexity as to who among these venerable recluses and brahmanas spoke the truth, and who spoke falsehood.

Unique in the history of religions, the Buddha revealed this answer:

Yes Kalamas, it is proper that you have doubt, that you have perplexity, for a doubt has arisen in a matter that is doubtful. Now, look you Kalamas, do not be led by reports, or tradition, or hearsay. Be not led by the authority of religious texts, nor by mere logic or inference, nor by considering appearances, nor by delight in speculative opinions, nor by seeming possibilities, nor by the idea: 'this is our teacher'. But, O Kalamas, when you know for yourselves that certain things are unwholesome and wrong and bad, then give them up... And when you know for yourselves that certain things are wholesome and good, then accept them and follow them.

The Buddha even told the monks and nuns that a disciple should examine the Tathagata (Buddha) himself or any other teacher, so that the disciple might be fully convinced of the true value of the teacher whom he followed.

It's O.K. to 'spy on your teacher' to be sure that they walk their talk. It could take years before you accept a teacher. In our information age, the need for a teacher one-on-one is less now than before because of dharma DVDs, the Internet, CDs, books and lecture tours. Still, it is best to have a teacher because they can save you a lot of time by pointing out the way, what you are doing wrong and telling you what you need to hear. My meditation really deepened after Ajahn Sona became my teacher in 2000 and he has constantly clarified the teachings of the Buddha for me. I am so thankful for this as I am a truth seeker. I want to know what did the Buddha really teach?

Buddha taught that it is wise to pay attention to the advice of elders in the sangha if you have them, but he did not want a strongly centralized religion with powerful authority figures because that would lead to ego problems. The Buddha gave an astonishing amount of freedom to his disciples to figure out the truth for themselves. In one of his last discourses the Buddha told his faithful attendant Ananda "After I have passed away, go to no other as your refuge. Let my teaching be your only guide. Be an island unto yourself. Go to no other as your guide." As Deepak Chopra says "The single biggest enemy of your spiritual life is organized religion."

The Path

The Buddhist path can be described as three inseparable stages: virtue, mental purification, and insight. The purpose of virtue or morality from a Buddhist view is to foster an environment by which you can concentrate your mind. This is very important to understand. In many religions, the purpose of morality is to be good, and not be bad. It is God's law so it is enforced with a heavy handed approach. If you sin, you will go to hell. The Buddhist approach is different and not so heavy handed. In Buddhism morality or discipline, has a future. You're going somewhere with it. Once you settle your life down with proper behaviour, you can sit and meditate and build up concentration in your mind. It is this concentration that naturally leads to the fruit of insight. Insight is a natural psychosomatic result that comes from a concentrated mind. This is not a belief system. This is direct experience. It's like water rising in a dam. The water rising is the concentration aspect, as in meditation. When the water reaches the top of the dam, you can use that power for electricity, which is insight. That's Buddhism.

The Four Noble Truths

This is the traditional starting point for a study of Buddhist philosophy. When the Buddha was 35 years old, several weeks after his great enlightenment he gave his first formal discourse in Deer Park in

Isipatanna, in northeastern India. He gave it to his five former ascetic friends who had practiced with him before. They stepped onto the pages of history when they became the Buddha's first monks, and the Buddha's first teaching to them was his insights into what he called the middle way, the avoidance of the extremes of sensuous indulgence and the extreme of self mortification or denial. Then he explained the four noble truths:

1. There is dukkha, suffering.
2. The cause of suffering is unwholesome desire.
3. There is an end to suffering, nirvana.
4. There is a way to the end of suffering, which is the noble eight-fold path.

'Noble' as it is used here, means an all pervasive truth that is as true as the law of gravity. Gravity is true whether you believe in it or not. Whether you understand gravity or not, or agree with gravity, or if it is not convenient for you at this time, if you jump off a ten story building, you will go splat on the pavement. Anywhere in the universe there is gravity and the four noble truths. That is what is meant by a noble truth.

Dukkha is one of those Pali and Sanskrit terms that cannot be properly translated into English. Pali is the oldest Buddhist language. Theravada Buddhists (the southern school) like to think that the Buddha spoke in Pali, but no one is sure about that. Pali is the language of the canonical scriptures of Theravada Buddhism and Sanskrit is the language of the northern school of Buddhism, or Mahayana. Basically, Buddhism went south and it went north from India. Dukkha translates as suffering but it has a much wider meaning than that. It also means impermanence, insubstantiality, change-ability, unsatisfactoriness and transitoriness. Everything in samsara is of the nature of dukkha. Anything that is made will fall apart and crumble and die, including the physical universe. The first noble truth is that life is suffering, dukkha. The Buddha's point is — understand dukkha and accept it. Accept reality. This is the nature of reality. Buddha gave us the bad news first. I had a lesson in the first noble truth of impermanence when I was hiking near Mount Baker in Washington. Our guide, Ty, was helping us explore an old mining shaft. After we left, as we hiked down the path he explained the geology of the area and Ty said "The idea that planet Earth has a natural balance, an inherent harmony, which always gently brings it back to normal, is just bad science. The evidence proves that Earth has gone through radical changes constantly, and the last 10,000 years is just one snap shot during this brief period of relative calm." So, even the crust of the earth where we live is impermanent in it's short term stability and reliability.

There was a famous American philosopher in the 1970s who eloquently described the first noble truth. She said, "There's always something!" This was when Gilda Radner, as Rosane Rosanadana on Saturday Night Live. As the years rolled by, long after she died, I finally realized what Rosane Rosanadana meant for us to understand. Her teaching is that there's always something messing up. There's always something going wrong. When Rosane Rosanadana contemplated the reality of all of the suffering in the world, she often remarked, "I thought I was gonna die!" Rosana was telling us to face the facts of the first noble truth of dukkha: no matter how beautiful and wonderful you are, something is going to fall apart in your life.

Another great philosopher was George Bernard Shaw, who said, "There are two great disappointments in life. One is not getting what you want, and the other is getting it." The second noble truth taught by the Buddha is that the cause of our suffering is unwholesome desire, which translates to mean thirst, clinging, attachment, grasping, craving, addiction, obsessive compulsive behaviours of all kinds. The root of suffering is "the pursuit of happiness." We each have a nagging itch that is a constant pull away from the present moment. That is desire. Desire itself does not have to be painful but when desire becomes attachment it is painful. The pleasure of what we enjoy is lost by coveting more. Desire persists. You only lose what you cling to. An example of clinging can be found in monkeys in Africa. Foreign zoos and zoological societies buy monkeys that are caught by people who put nuts in glass jars. The jars have very narrow openings and are weighed down so heavily that monkeys can't move them. They come in the morning and spread out many of these jars on the jungle floor, then they go back and play cards all day. At the end of the day they come and find many monkeys trapped by the jars. The monkeys reach in for the nuts but they can't take their hands out with their fists full. Their monkey brains don't tell them that they just have to let go of their clinging to be free. So unharmed, they are captured and sent away. When people go to see their best friend to talk about their problems, it's like they are holding on to a jar with one hand. Their best friend may tell them to let go of their problem, or their friend may polish their jar and encourage their clinging.

One criticism of the Buddha is the question, "If the Buddha didn't have any desires, then why did he teach? Isn't that a desire? Isn't doing compassionate action for people a form of desire?" Well, there are wholesome and unwholesome desires. It's OK to have wholesome desires. The Buddha didn't have any unwholesome desires. It's like using a needle to take out a sliver. Once you've got the sliver out you don't keep poking away with the needle. So that's not a mystery at all. Consider right effort, number six on the eightfold path. Effort means to have an aspiration and to put forth energy and exertion and to rub up against your habitual desires, to go against your habitual desires. For example, a married man may have the habitual pattern of pursuing sexually arousing women which results in extramarital affairs. But then he hears the Buddha's precept to not engage in sexual misconduct. He's at a client's office party and he meets a woman who's presence causes him to trigger his habitual response. But his effort in this case is to look at his own lust, to look at his own mind. He slowly turns away from her and reaches for some broccoli and dip. He holds himself back. So, in this example, the man's sexual desire arose and then it was his effort that broke him out of his instinctual habitual pattern. So negative desire is bad, effort is good. When the Buddha chose to get up and teach he was not acting out of clinging, attachment or craving desire. He chose to apply effort out of compassion for others.

The third noble truth is that there is a cessation to suffering. It is called nirvana, the final ultimate enlightenment. Unless someone told you, how would you know there actually is such a thing? A state of no mental or emotional suffering, a state beyond suffering. There can still be physical discomfort but without the unhappy emotional state that goes with that. Nirvana or nibbana in Pali, is a permanent deathless state beyond the struggles of samsara. Enlightenment is the transcendence of the self, or self limitation. It is the discarding of the ego. The word nirvana translates literally as 'blown out.' Meaning, the ego is blown out. After that, there is no longer any possibility of ever slipping back into the sleep of ego ever again. You are awake!

The fourth noble truth is that there is a path which will lead a practitioner to the end of suffering. This path is what the Buddha taught. He described it as the noble eightfold path because there are eight aspects to the path. They are practiced together, not in any particular order. The most universal symbol of the Buddhist religion is the wheel. It is represented with eight spokes and it is said that the Buddha first turned the wheel of dharma during that discourse to the five monks in Deer Park. This is the dharmachakra sutta, which means the turning of the wheel discourse. Just about everything the Buddha taught for 45 years was aspects of this eightfold path.

Those are the four noble truths, which is a concise description of the Buddha's message. After the Buddha's enlightenment he realized that nirvana cannot be taught. He said that enlightenment is impossible to describe but he did give 43 adjectives to describe it, like: no greed, no hatred, no delusion. It is luminous and permanent, whereas everything in samsara is impermanent. It is a direct experience that can only be comprehended once you're there. The Buddha was sitting beside a

A Short Walk On An Ancient Path

lotus pond when he hesitated about teaching people at all. His mind inclined away from teaching. At that moment a Brahma realm brahma read the Buddha's mind and he thought "The world is lost. The world will perish. The Buddha will not teach." The brahmas are higher than the devas. Then, in one of history's heroic acts, this brahma disappeared from that world and appeared before the Buddha. He pleaded with the Buddha to teach and he encouraged him by pointing out that there were some people who could understand his teachings. Finally, the Buddha agreed to teach. Satisfied and very happy, the brahma disappeared and went back up to heaven.

At that time the Buddha contemplated the lotus pond and he realized that human beings are like lotus flowers. Some are like a lotus under the mud, others thrive their entire life under the water. But when the lotus flower comes out of the water and blooms, that is symbolic of enlightened mind. So the Buddha chose the lotus flower as the symbol of enlightened mind. He said that there are a few people with little dust in their eyes, who would be able to penetrate to the truth of the way things are. Today, you can see a lot of lotus flowers in Buddhist temples. If the Buddha had been sitting in a field of dandelions at that particular time, history may have been quite different.

When the Buddha decided to teach he realized that he could only teach the way to nirvana. This is an important understanding. The Buddha concerned himself with teaching people the practical steps to proceed along the spiritual path. He wasn't interested in giving them the knowledge of the universe which he knew but took to the grave. He taught people how to get to enlightenment so that they could attain this ultimate direct experience themselves. Buddhism is a practical path of ethics, mindfulness, awareness and meditation practices designed to clear away our ignorance and confusion so that we can see the true nature of reality. Buddhism is not about the experience of nirvana. Buddhism has more to do with paying attention to your hands when you are polishing your shoes, than it has to do with a holy spiritual experience. Buddhism is the way to nirvana, but once you've made it, you can let go of Buddhism the way you let go of a jet after it has flown you across the ocean.

The Buddha

'Buddha' is a title given to the first man that attains enlightenment in his age, and teaches it to others. This first person cannot be a woman. They must be a man. This doesn't go over well with the feminists but we cannot deny that this is clearly stated in the suttas. Certainly the Buddha expounded that women have attained to arahantship but perhaps one reason why the first great leader can't be a woman is because India was one of the most sexist countries, then as now. Because such men are so ignorant they are probably incapable of respecting a female Buddha enough, so therefore it would make sense for each Buddha to be a man. The word 'Buddha' comes from the root words 'Bud' or 'Bodhi' which means 'awake,' and 'dha' meaning 'man.' Buddha means awakened man. His family name was Prince Siddhartha Gotama. He was the crown prince of the Sakya kingdom. That's why Mahayanists call him Sakyamuni Buddha. 'Muni' means 'sage,' sage of the Sakyas. His father was King Suddhodana, a virtuous king, deserving of a child like prince Siddhartha. The Buddha wasn't the Buddha until age 35. He was born in modern day Nepal near the Indian border, as best we can tell. India at that time was a feudal society. The Buddha lived and taught throughout about ten of these feudal kingdoms. Each one was maybe 100 or 200 kilometres across. Very much unlike Jesus Christ, the Buddha was loved by the political powers of his day Jesus was faced with a monolithic and mean Roman Empire. The Buddha could divide and conquer so to speak, so he had it easier. The Buddha said that he chose the proper causes and conditions into which to take birth, to become the next Buddha. Why did Jesus choose to be born on the wrong side of the tracks? Compassion for that part of the Roman Empire, perhaps?

The Buddha became a pop idol soon after launching his career into the big time. They didn't have sunglasses in those days, but he was surrounded by his retinue. Kings would supplicate the Buddha to come and visit their kingdom. "Please come and spend the rainy season retreat in our kingdom. We'll donate a beautiful new monastery for your monks and nuns if you will please bless us with your presence!" they might say.

As a child Prince Siddhartha was a child prodigy and he grew up in luxury. His father wanted him to take over the throne, as Siddhartha was his first son. The King fed him with consorts to indulge him in sensuous pleasure because the king didn't want his son to get any spiritual ideas about becoming a monk and giving up the kingdom. At age 16 the prince married the princess Yasodhara from the kingdom of Kosala and she was a very spiritual and devoted wife. They would go around the kingdom together like John and Yoko, trying to better the lives of the poor. When he was 29 they had one baby boy, Rahula. Just after this, with his wife's support, Prince Siddhartha renounced the worldly life of the palace and ran away from home one night. He fled over the river into the next kingdom of Magadha so that his daddy, the king, couldn't come and take him back. King Suddhodana was very sad but prince Siddhartha was free. He became a monk, studied under two leading pre-Hindu teachers, then broke off on his own to find his own way to enlightenment. He had his own confusion too, but Siddhartha had the gift to ask questions. When he was sitting under a pipala tree (later renamed the bodhi tree in his honour) along the Neranjara river early one morning, he attained to full and complete enlightenment. The rest, as they say, is history.

Central Shrine at War Xieng Thong, northern Laos

Chapter 2

How to Meditate

"Let us begin."

In this extemporaneous exposition, Venerable Sona guides us in a simple yet insightful way through the fundamentals of breath meditation practice. Using the method taught by the Buddha as a framework he leads the reader in the direction of clarity and stillness, this clarity and stillness allows us to investigate the nature of reality, truth, and goodness.

Meditation on Breathing
By Ajahn Sona

Meditation on breathing is one of the most widely practiced of Buddhist meditation techniques. It was devised and developed by the Buddha himself, and He taught it during his lifetime. For 2500 years it has been widely studied both by monks and laypeople.

Breath meditation has many virtues. It is simple and portable — your breath goes with you wherever you go. It will be with you until your last breath. The breath is neither a fascinating, attractive nor interesting object; it is not a repulsive object. It is neutral.

The breath is observed through contact. It is not visual; it is felt. The location to focus on — which is given by the Buddha himself in several discourses in which he described the meditation — is at the entrance to the body. The breath enters the body at the nostrils or the mouth. Some people have conditions where they must breathe through their mouth, if they have a cold, for example. They need not abandon breathing meditation. Contact of the breath at the lip is also a possible site — although it is difficult to feel the inhalation there. But primarily the breath is felt at the nose.

Begin by paying attention to the coolness of the inhalation inside the nostrils. The Buddha makes a simile that mindfulness is similar to a sentry at the entrance to a walled city. The sentry is posted at the entrance. He does not have to know who is inside the city and who is outside. All he has to know is that there is just one way in and out of that city, and that is the entranceway. Therefore, he guards the entrance in the same way mindfulness observes the entrance of the breath. It does not follow it inside the body. It does not concern itself with the outside of the body. It merely acts as a sentry. All the air coming into the body or going out of the body must pass through the nostrils. So we post mindfulness at the nostrils.

The same qualities we value a sentry for, we value mindfulness for at the nostrils: alertness, constancy, non-distraction, non-sleepiness, non-agitation, and inability to be bribed. Being bribed is like asking your mind to pay attention to the breath, and then seeing other more enticing thoughts and images come along. You may be bribed into paying attention to those, rather than to the breath. The sentry should not be easily bought off. You have to refuse the offers of more tantalizing images, thoughts, plans and reveries. You must strictly observe the breath at the entrance of the body.

One should not be over-rigid and excessively zealous, otherwise this produces agitation. Neither should you be drifting off into sleep — too relaxed. You need the middle ground, a balance between tension and drifting away. Feel the coolness of the inhalation. Feel the warmth of the exhalation.

The Buddha advises we pay attention to the duration of the breath. Is it a long breath, or is it a short breath? He doesn't ask you to control your breath or your breathing; merely to breathe naturally and unselfconsciously. You should observe and not interfere. But note a long breath when one occurs on an inhalation or an exhalation, and a short breath when one occurs on an inhalation or an exhalation.

When your mind has established itself and is able to pay attention long enough to observe whether or not it is a long or short breath, then you can ask it to do something a little more challenging, as the mind may wander and still know whether it is a long breath or a short breath.

A Short Walk On An Ancient Path

Now, the Buddha asks that we observe the beginning, the middle and the end of each breath, both the inhalation and the exhalation. In other words, the entire duration of the breath from its beginning to its end. This is a new demand on mindfulness: that the sentry observes every detail of what is passing in and out of that entrance. The sentry's attention must be constant, not wandering at all. It is a more demanding level of practice.

If you find the mind occasionally wanders — which is very common and to be expected — one should not feel frustrated or a failure at this normal action of the mind. Instead, simply notice when your attention has wandered and start the exercise again, noticing the beginning, the middle and the end of each breath.

This exercise itself should not produce excess tension or a hypnotic effect. It is an attempt to increase alertness, awareness and the capacity to sustain attention. If you succeed, you will feel a very great sense of clarity, presence, and lack of distraction. You will not feel in the least bored, agitated, irritated, nor will you feel in doubt. You will be confidently observing the flow of breath in this very lucid condition.

You will be aware of precisely what you are doing. This is the first benefit of this exercise, that one experiences well-being here and now. You have dispelled the variety of hindrances or negative mental states that occur in the ordinary mind: ill will, sensual fantasies or obsessions, agitation, sloth and drowsiness, and indecision or problematic doubting. By observing the breath, one is delivered from these negative mental states.

Proceeding further, one may begin to notice a subtle change, taking place at the very point of contact where the breath meets the nostrils. It may turn from a flowing sensation — a cottony flow of air gently against the nostrils — to a static pressure, a light, airy but motionless effect. It is as if light cotton batten is being touched to the nostrils. This is a sign that the mind is becoming very focused, still and calm. The object, the breath, begins to take on the quality of stillness rather than motion. This is a sign of increasing concentration, increasing focus, and increasing stillness of mind.

At this point the aches and pains in one's body tend to dissolve. The body is not troubled, and experiences a rather pleasant sensation. The mind also experiences a pleasant sensation of being undistracted, calm, strong, even, present, alert, and untroubled.

Now, one may turn one's attention to the topic of the impermanent nature of this process, or the impermanent nature of all phenomena, or the substanceless nature of the breath. Since it is a flow, there is nothing enduring or substantial to it. Noticing this characteristic in the breath, one can also notice this characteristic in all sense objects — whatever one sees, hears, smells, tastes, touches and thinks. All are flowing; all are insubstantial.

The mind in this rested, very alert state, when asked to investigate the flowing nature of reality, will often perceive it with greater impact than in normal distracted states of consciousness. It will be less preoccupied with this flowing world, or realize that since all things in the world are flowing, they cannot be grasped, held or controlled. They do not last. When the mind sees this characteristic, this sign, it relaxes its grip and its futile attempt to control, to grasp, and to hold. This is one of the direct benefits of calming the mind through breath meditation, turning the attention to the flowing quality of the breath, and then further, to the flowing quality of all phenomena.

You may also wish to go deeper into tranquility by focusing the mind on the still quality of the breath, that is, this cottony characteristic where the breath contacts the nostrils. When that becomes very, very still, this is an indication that the mind is stilling. By continuing to focus without too great a tension and without relaxation, in an alert way, one goes deeper into stillness, clarity, and a profound well-being. There is a lack of pain in the body, a decrease of pleasant feelings in the body, and an increase of joy.

This is in the direction of profound concentration, the eighth factor of the Noble Eightfold Path. Do not expect to enter this state without a good deal of preparation, without a good deal of refinement in your life. It requires a great deal of sensitivity and refinement of the mind. On the other hand, do not think it impossible to calm the mind, to produce clarity and stillness in the mind. It is possible for the ordinary person to develop. Given enough patience and time and correct practice, one may learn the great value of breath meditation.

Breath meditation is something that can unfold during the entire lifetime. It becomes one's best friend. It becomes a refuge. It becomes an unending source of clarity and stillness from which to base investigation into the nature of reality, the nature of truth, the nature of goodness. It is an

A Short Walk On An Ancient Path

invaluable aid to awakening, taught by the Buddha himself, practiced by the Buddha himself, and recommended by twenty-five centuries of teachers of meditation.

I leave you with these instructions. May you be well, happy, and peaceful.

(Transcription by Donna Woods.)

Commentary

Adding to these wise words of Ajahn Sona: when you sit down to meditate it is important to sit upright. Don't lean back on anything, except maybe your hip in the back of a chair. Relax into it; you should not feel strained. Think of yourself as a puppet with the string coming out of the top of your head. Or imagine your spine as a stack of neatly piled golden coins, or a stack of dinner plates. If you lean way back on a chair there's a big danger of falling asleep. Ideally, sit cross-legged on the ground. You can use a chair if your legs aren't so supple, and keep your legs straight if that is comfortable. If your legs fall asleep you can mindfully move them. Some people think meditation is boot camp and they are supposed to endure as much pain as they can, but this is not so. You should sit on a cushion about six inches thick. Unless you have been raised in a culture in which you're used to sitting flat on the floor, you will need to use something to raise your buttocks six to eight inches above your legs. You may prefer a wider cushion, almost a square meter in size which will allow you to sit and also rest your feet and ankles on the cushion. Or you could use a separate cushion for your ankles.

Complete your posture by placing your hands lightly, together in your lap, or palms down on your thighs, or anyway that is comfortable. In Theravada Buddhism we generally meditate with our eyes closed as there is less distraction but if you get sleepy you can open them a crack, looking down. The light coming in helps to keep you awake. If you're not sleepy, it's better to keep the eyes closed to cut out sensory distraction.

In the book *No Ajahn Chah – Reflections,* he said (Chah, 1994; 20)

"Time is our present breath." You follow the breath going in and out at the nostrils. That is the object of your meditation. There is a natural gap between breaths. If it helps to use words, during the in-breath you can mentally say to yourself "in-breath" and during the out-breath you say "out-breath." The words are like training wheels for the mind; they help you keep your mind on what you're doing while you're doing it because they displace other discursive thoughts. Just allow your breathing to be natural. Do not try to interfere with it in any way. Sometimes it is shallow, sometimes deep. Be mindful because there is a natural tendency to control the breath once you start to focus your attention on it.

As you sit, very soon you will be distracted by a thought, any thought. You may have a thought about the past or fantasies about the future. At that point you just ignore the thought, try to let it go, and come back to the breath. Whatever arises in the five senses of seeing, hearing, feeling, smelling and tasting, you just let those go as well. Try not to space out but of course we all do, so just be gentle with yourself and come back. Come back to your breath. Ram Dass practiced meditation in Burma and he said "When you're meditating you can visualize your thoughts as autumn leaves floating down a stream, and your mind is the stream itself. Some leaves are brighter than others, with speckles of water on them but let them all go. If you pick up a leaf and hang onto it then you're just thinking, not meditating." You can visualize that image from time to time if it helps you to let go of your thoughts. I've used that image on thousands of people during guided meditations in my courses.

Extra techniques that you can try in your meditation, if you need them, are you can notice the coolness of the breath on the nostrils on the inhalation, then the breath is warmed by the body and you notice the warmth on the nostrils on the exhalation. How many millions of breaths have people taken? When I point that out some reply, "Say! I've never thought about that before!" You can also count the breaths. You

A Short Walk On An Ancient Path

note, "one" on the inhalation, "two" on the exhalation", then "three" in, "four" out, counting up to ten, then go back to one. If you lose your count, just go back to one. Counting is like a thread that joins the breath together so it makes it easier, it gives you something to do to keep you occupied. Just following the breath in and out is difficult to do, isn't it? The technique is simple but the mind is so complicated.

Another practice is to label your thoughts by saying to yourself "thinking". This gives you some leverage to come back to your breath. Just say "thinking," then go back to the breath. "Thinking", back to the breath. The labelling technique means that you label your thoughts and your five senses. This is mindfulness/ awareness. You are aware of what is arising in your mind. It's like crap shooting. "Seeing," pow! "Hearing," pow! "Thinking," pow! "Feeling," pow! Whatever comes up, you blast it, or note it. Don't space out. You can use this technique when your thoughts are tumbling and rumbling but if the mind is calm it's best to let go of all the words and just be with the peace. So do it just when you need to but you shouldn't be labelling all the time.

A mantra is also a useful technique. When your mind is so distracted that you can't stay with the breath, you can repeat a meditation word. Mantra means "mind protection". You repeat a word on the inhalation to knock out your thoughts. Then you repeat another word or the same word on the exhalation. You can even visualize the letters of the word in white letters. Then visualize the next word in yellow letters, or whatever. This uses the sense of sight, sound and sub vocalization. By engaging your senses in this way you dominate the mind so as to knock out the discursive thoughts. Then, when you get some handle on your mind, you can drop the mantra and go back to the breath again.

I encourage you to experiment with all of these techniques to make your meditation work. The Tao says that you should facilitate what actually is happening, rather than stick to what you expect to happen. Another practice is to bring your awareness into your body and scan your sensations. Whatever pulls your mind out of your thoughts and into the body is good. You should regularly review how the body is positioned because you are synchronizing your body, speech and mind in meditation. This is precise inner work and hard inner work.

Take a working man's approach. To always connect your mind to your body will keep you in reality. I took flying lessons and my instructor told me forcefully "You steer the plane. You don't let it steer you!" In meditation you steer your thoughts rather than allowing them to steer you . Meditation is not spacing out. You are being present, looking into yourself, into your heart. If you want to know what something is like, you observe it. If you want to know what the mind is like, you observe the mind, watch the thoughts. As you look at your mind, there's nothing else happening, just your breath and your deepest innermost being churning around, unravelling your confusion.

You can have your mouth slightly open with your tongue touching the palate, the roof of your mouth. This reduces salivation and it prevents you from unconsciously clenching your jaw. Frequently bring your attention to your posture, to your head and shoulders. Some people end up leaning over a few inches. Try to sit still because it's good for building concentration, but if you have to move because of physical discomfort, move mindfully. Buddhism is the middle way. We work ourselves hard, but not too hard. It's good to make minor adjustments in your position to overcome pain.

When you're meditating, don't blame yourself for having a constantly wandering mind. Everyone feels that way, because everyone is that way. Your mind is not hopeless! The Buddha insisted that your mind is a workable situation. You can do it! You can meditate. It takes practice, like any other skill or craft that you have learned. All anyone can do for you is to bring you to the beginning of the eightfold path. You must choose to tread that path, and do the rest yourself. Sangha is there to help keep you on track, but you must do your own work. What matters is getting yourself to the cushion in the first place, and then doing your practice. The actual technique that you choose to practice is one thing but having the discipline to do that practice is another. Discipline is the basis of all virtue so keep regular. Stay with your meditation practice as humble as it is. It is wise to have one or two main practices of meditation such as breath and loving kindness. With that established, you can add other Buddhist contemplations and meditations such as the contemplations on dana- generosity, death and impermanence, precious human birth, karma, considering the shortcomings of samsara, the recollection of deities and others. During the day reflect upon the view. When you're not meditating you still live within the world view of the dhamma and refine your view. The Buddha had big plans for us. He spent the first seven weeks after his enlightenment planning how he would present his message to devas and men, and then he proclaimed himself boldly.

Meditating puts us in tune with our being, with experiencing our life as it ordinarily is. Ajahn Sona said:

> Sometimes when people see someone sitting with their legs crossed and their eyes closed they think they are very remote from the way we function in the world but actually what we're trying to do is gain a very heightened state of realism. Most people are very unrealistic. They think they have a job and raise a family and they're very realistic but they're not realistic at all. They are out of touch with reality.

You should meditate everyday, ideally for one hour. You can start with as little as ten minutes per day, but try to get it up to 30, 40, and even 60 minutes. You don't have to do it all at once, or at any set time per day, but it probably works better to pick one time in your schedule to meditate, or you might skip it. Mornings are good because your nerves are a bit more refreshed after you've slept. You can wake yourself up, have a shower and a cup of coffee, then meditate. Don't sit right after a meal because you'll get sleepy. The Buddha taught his monks and nuns to go for a walk after a meal. Ayya Khema taught "Meditation is a very important thing to do, like flossing your teeth." She was a German Buddhist nun and the most famous Western nun. Her books and talks are a treasure.

Someone once told the Dalai Lama that they were living a good life, they followed all the precepts, they cared about others and had compassion. So, they asked the Dalai Lama, what could they possibly do next? Immediately the Dalai Lama said "Mental stabilization." What the Dalai Lama meant by this is that the next stage after living a moral life, is to stabilize the mind in meditation practice. Meditation practices are the essential steps along the path to enlightenment. The Buddha recommended a balance of practice and study. So, let's get into some meditation practice now. The definition of meditation in one sentence is that meditation means to pay attention in a particular way. This means to familiarize your mind constantly and thoroughly with a virtuous object. In the meditation technique which we will do, you pay attention to your in and out breath at the tip of the nose. Meditation works with our wandering thoughts in an effort to train the mind with mindfulness and awareness, to stay in the present moment and move the mind toward tranquility and serenity. Meditation can clear away our confusion and stress, and help purify our minds. Meditators often secretly believe that they are the worst meditators in the world but everybody has a neurotic wandering mind. I remember when my father got me into meditation. He took me on my first meditation retreat in 1974. It was at a beautiful location on Niagara-on-the-Lake and I was the only 14 year old in the group. I thought that maybe I was too immature to do the practice properly because my thoughts kept wandering all over the place. Then we had a group discussion and everybody else was saying the same thing about the difficulties they were having with thoughts chattering away on the inside of their skulls. That was a revelation and an encouragement that I wasn't any worse than the other meditators so I kept at it.

It is good for meditators to share their experience with a teacher and get some experienced feedback. It's also an uplifting feeling to meditate in a group. It would be good to find a group to sit with once a week, or form your own group. Sangha is the Buddhist word for community. Not only are people crying out for some sense of community, but the Buddhist teachings indicate that the path to enlightenment is easier with a sangha. The three jewels are: the Buddha, the dharma and the sangha. Ananda once remarked to the Buddha, "Having good friends to practice with is half of the spiritual life." "Not so Ananda," the Buddha replied. "Having good friends to practice with is all of the spiritual life." It is a blessing to have a good teacher, or a group of monks and nuns at the core of a sangha. You are still responsible for working out your own understanding. It is a disempowering model to have students relying on a teacher so the Buddha did not want his monks to depend upon him. He taught that you must work out the truth for yourself. In the Tao Te Ching, Lao Tzu taught that the second greatest leaders are loved by the people but the greatest leaders of all are hardly noticed by the people.

A good book providing 101 more techniques for meditation is, *Mindfulness in Plain English,* by Bhante Gunaratana. You can get it or download it for free off the net.

Vipassana Meditation

There is a fair bit of confusion around vipassana meditation. Buddhist meditation is a process of samatha-vipassana. Samatha means calm, vipassana means insight or clear seeing with the eye of wisdom — clear seeing about the truth of the way things are. The Buddha almost always hyphenated the term. He almost never used the word vipassana on its own. Vipassana is the result of a process. Samatha-vipassana are two sides of the same coin. Ajahn Chah taught that "They go together, they always go together, they must go together." This is taught in the Theravada Forest tradition because we are following the Buddha. Over time some groups have separated the two as two different kinds of meditation going in two different directions. Vipassana has been separated from Buddhism itself as "the vipassana religion." Ajahn Viradhammo said "The word 'vipassana' is not that important a word in Theravada Buddhism." Today Vipassana has become a brand name and people think they are practicing that but the Buddha taught an eightfold path — not just meditation. The whole path needs to be practiced, not just some specialized vipassana techniques. Within vipassana there are different technique schools with over excessive advocacy of one technique. This gets misleading and confusing. Go back and read what the Buddha taught about how to meditate. It's OK to call breath meditation Vipassana meditation because the people who are using the vipassana brand name are doing breath meditation as well. Whole Vipassana schools are based upon the Satipattana sutta, which is a composite of several suttas combined by the Theravadin fathers to make "the longest discourse" on how to meditate. In it the Buddha teaches how to connect with reality but he didn't specify precisely about whether meditation practice had to be just this way, or that way. Lord Buddha gave us the parameters by saying for example, "When a monk has a thought, he knows he has a thought." Ajahn Sucitto from Chithurst Monastery in England said "Meditation is not just about sitting, it's weather the mind can be skilful" (Sucitto, 2002; 23).

Ajahn Lee Meditation Method

Below is another meditation method from the forest tradition. This comes from Ajahn Lee who was a disciple of Ajahn Mun. In the West this practice has been introduced by Ajahn Thanissaro from the Metta Forest Monastery, at watmetta.org . What is interesting about this practice is that instead of holding your attention to the breath at the tip of the nose, you imagine breathing into different parts of your body. This moves your attention around and seems to make it easier to pay attention to what you are doing because you are busy feeling the breath energy here and there. The whole body gives you a wider object to bring your attention back to. You can use this method for walking meditation as well. For more more detailed instructions on this technique of breath meditation go to www.accesstoinsight.org. These guided breath meditation instructions were given by Ajahn Thanissaro.

Close your eyes and start your meditation by concentrating on the breath. When the mind strays, come back to your breath. Come back to the present moment.

So what have you got here? You've got the breath coming in and out. You've got the body sitting right here breathing and you've got the mind, which is thinking and aware. What you want to do is bring all those things together. Think about the breath coming in and going out. And then be aware of the breath as it's coming in, as it's going out. Be aware of how the breathing feels. Allow yourself to breathe in whatever way feels most comfortable. It's good to start with some good deep long in-and-out breaths to see if long breathing does feel good for you. As long as it feels comfortable, maintain that rhythm.

If it's feeling uncomfortable or strenuous, you can try shorter breathing. Deep breathing, shallow breathing, heavy, light, fast, slow: experiment with different rhythms of breathing to see which one feels most comfort-able. Think of the breathing as a whole body process. The whole body breathes in together, the whole body breathes out together. Try to notice, when you breathe in, which parts of the body do you tend to tense up? Or when you breathe out are there any parts of the body where you tend to hold onto any tension? And then let yourself relax. When you breathe out just let the tension go out with the breath. And when you breathe in you realize you don't have to tense up the body to breathe in. The breath will come in anyway. It will come in even more comfortably if you don't tense up the body.

When the breathing process feels comfortable, start to explore how the breathing process feels in different parts of the body. A good place to start is around the naval. Just notice where that part of the body is in your awareness right now. Locate that part of the body, then watch it as you breathe in and breathe out. See how it feels. If you notice any ten-sion or tightness or unevenness in the breath there, think of it relaxing, smoothing out, dissolving away. If you want, you can even think of the energy of the breathing process coming in and out of the body right there at the naval, dissolving away any tension you may feel.

Now move your attention up to the solar plexus and follow the same three steps there.

1. Locate that general part of the body in your awareness right now. You don't have to be too specific.
2. Notice how it feels in that part of the body as you breathe in and breathe out.
3. If you feel any tension — say a build up of tension as you breathe in, a holding between the in-breath and the out-breath, or holding on as you breathe out — just let it relax. Breathe in, breathe out, in a way that feels good for that part of the body. Whatever rhythm feels best for that part of the body, let the breath come in-and-out at that rhythm.

If there's any pain just let it be. There's a difference between tension and pain. You can breathe into tension to dissolve it but pain you may not be able to affect. Just let pain be.

After a few minutes move to the middle of your chest…

Then the bottom of your throat…

Then breathe into the centre of your forehead between the eyebrows and breathe in from the back of the head. Be gentle here, for this is an area we tend to use too much. You can breathe into the sides of your head and the top of your head. Feel the breath energy flowing through your head and around your body. You can imagine that you are breathing in your ears and out your ears or breathing in your eyes and out your eyes.

Now, you can continue the survey of the body at your own pace, by breathing in from the back of your neck and around the shoulders past the arms to the tips of the fingers. When the in-breath starts imagine it going straight to the fingertips and then you can breathe out wherever you like. Then later, breathe in the back of the neck and go down the back, out the legs to the tips of the toes, in the same way. Just go through the body, section by section, and notice how it feels in each section as you breathe in and breathe out. If you feel any tension or tightness or discomfort in the breathing process, just let it relax, so it feels like breath energy is going in comfortably, and out comfortably, right there. And then move on.

You can go through the body as many times as you like but if you feel after a while that you'd like to settle down on just one spot, choose any

A Short Walk On An Ancient Path

one spot in the body where it's easy for the mind to stay centred. Just be with the breath at that spot and think of your awareness spreading out from that spot, like the light of a candle. The candle flame is at one spot but its light can fill a whole room. Think of your awareness spreading out from that one spot and filling your whole body the same way, and then see if you can maintain that expanded awareness. There's nowhere else you have to go right now, nothing else you have to do. Just be with the body breathing in and out. Think of the breath, be aware of the breath. Try to keep those things together as consistently as possible.

(Transcription by Brian Ruhe)

Meditation on Loving-kindness
By Ajahn Sona

The Buddha taught throughout his life that the practice of loving-kindness is central to happiness here and now, and happiness in the future. The practice of loving-kindness is a blameless practice. Its fruits are all positive. There are no negative by-products. The Buddha left us with several detailed discourses on loving-kindness and how to practice them.

The word 'loving-kindness' is an English translation of the word 'metta' which comes from the ancient Pali language. The word 'metta' has its roots in 'friendliness'. So friendliness is really what we're talking about when we speak of loving-kindness—a profound, deep friendliness towards other beings and towards oneself.

This quality of friendliness must be generated in the mind, cultivated and practiced often. People often feel that such emotions as loving-kindness or deep friendliness need to arise spontaneously, that they shouldn't be exercised, that they should just happen, or that they drop into your mind from heaven. But the Buddha emphasizes again and again that although this is a heavenly state—a sublime abiding, a divine condition of the mind and the heart—it happens *from* you and not *to* you. You are the maker of your own heaven.

When the Buddha gave the discourse on loving-kindness, it is very interesting to note that the first quarter of the teachings are preliminaries to loving-kindness — what has to be done before you can satisfactorily practice loving-kindness.

Detailing the preliminaries, he begins by saying, "This is what should be done by one who is skilled in goodness and who knows the path of peace." "Skilled in goodness" means we have to know what is skilful and what is unskilful thought, speech, and action. To "know the path of peace" is to know the Noble Eightfold Path, which explains skilful and unskilful speech and action. Therefore, this knowledge is required for the regulated generation of loving-kindness. It is the solid basis for the practice. It requires some wisdom and knowledge.

The Buddha continues, "Let them be able and upright, straightforward and gentle in speech." "Able and upright" is a kind of virtue, a kind of attitude. "Straightforward" is again a quality of character, a lack of deviance, a lack of cunning and conniving, being up-front and straightforward, but also "gentle in speech." The speech is true but beneficial. These are also the foundations for loving-kindness.

As a basis for practicing loving-kindness, one must also be "humble and not conceited", the Buddha continues. Humility means a lack of ego. It is a kind of flexibility. The grass is often compared to humility, while a brittle tree is compared to rigidity and conceit. When a strong wind blows, the brittle tree will break but the grass will bend and have no difficulty because it is low and flexible. So the low ego, the flexible personality, is not disturbed by reports from reality, either about themselves or about others, because they have not invested themselves with false dimensions or enlarged themselves inappropriately. They have little suffering.

The Buddha also mentions other prerequisites for loving-kindness. He says they are to be "contented and easily satisfied." Contentment and satisfaction allow room for the generation of an emotion like loving-kindness. If one is constantly filled with ambition and the tension that goes with ambition — the drive to accumulate, the drive to have power — it doesn't leave room for the peaceful, expansive nature of loving-kindness. These are two mutually exclusive mind states. To be discontented and demanding is opposed to the atmosphere of loving-kindness.

The Buddha then reminds us that those who wish to practice loving-kindness should be "unburdened with duties and frugal in their ways." In

A Short Walk On An Ancient Path

the household life, it is sometimes difficult to be unburdened with duties. In the monastic life, it is certainly an ideal to seek a simple life in a small cottage or meditation dwelling without too many duties. But this ideal is something also to be aspired to in the household life.

The Buddha is saying that one should not clutter one's life with frantic activity, thinking that the mere rushing about and doing things is wise or profitable. Rather, one should undertake duties that are proper, necessary and helpful to oneself and others but without merely distracting oneself continuously. The cultivation of loving-kindness requires an undistracted mind.

Frugality is one of the ways in which you can allow yourself to have more time, not to be reckless in spending money or in accumulating things. One should be modest and moderate, knowing what is appropriate and what is not, what is necessary and what is frivolous, so that the mind is not burdened. One then has time and space to cultivate what is truly lasting and truly valuable.

The Buddha then goes on to mention other skilful states for generating loving-kindness: "Peaceful and calm, and wise and skilful" Peace and calmness of mind are also foundations for the development of loving-kindness. And the reverse is also true: loving-kindness is also a foundation for peace and calm. So if you want to practice a calming meditation, quite often it is helpful to start with loving-kindness. And if you want to practice loving-kindness, it is often helpful to start with a calming meditation. They support each other mutually.

He goes on, "One should wish that *in gladness and safety, may all beings be at ease.*" This is the essential wish of loving-kindness or friendliness, that beings be glad, safe and at ease. When we send out loving-kindness, we may use phrases like, "May all beings be happy, may all beings be at peace, may all beings be safe, may all beings be at ease."

Then there is a series of categories. The Buddha makes sure that we include all beings without restriction. He says, "Whatever living beings that there may be, omitting none, weak or strong, great, medium, or small, the seen and the unseen, those living near or far away, the born and to be born (those in the womb), may all beings be at ease." And we wish, "Let beings not deceive each other, let them not despise other beings, let none through anger or ill, will wish harm upon another," so we wish that they also may have loving-kindness.

The final simile that sums up the picture that the Buddha paints is the beautiful line, "Even as a mother protects with her life her child, her only child, so with a boundless heart should one cherish all living beings, radiating kindness over the entire world: upwards to the skies, downward to the depths, outward, unbounded, without any ill will." So we have the simile of the affection of the mother for her only child, where she protects with her life her only child. This means one encourages the positive and discourages negativity. One should explore and dwell on the nature of the kindness a mother has for her only child.

The Buddha then describes how and when this should be practiced. "Whether standing, walking, seated or lying down, one should sustain this recollection." So the posture is not important. It is a thing that one does with one's mind, whether just before going to sleep or just upon waking up. Whether in the middle of the day, at work, sitting quietly in the forest, in the meditation room with a group or whether alone, one can practice, "one can sustain this recollection." So one can recollect one's attitude throughout the day.

"This is said to be the sublime abiding." A heaven here and now is cultivated and generated through one's own mind. And it is through one's own mind, and no other way, that one produces the refinement of consciousness, which corresponds to heaven. The loving-kindness meditation answers many needs and wants in our lives. But it is our responsibility to generate this. It is not dependent on who loves us. It is dependent on us generating love unconditionally for others.

So in meditation you may bring up the image and feeling of a mother's love for her only child, radiating it outward from oneself to other beings. Or you may begin with other beings, radiating loving-kindness towards oneself. You can begin with beings you have a natural affection for, and radiate it slowly outward to those more distant from you, or you can radiate loving-kindness to the vast universe itself.

These are all suggestions and techniques. There are no rules for this. All we want to understand is, does it work? And what works well for me? Images, poems, and songs — all of these things may work for different

A Short Walk On An Ancient Path

people. One should explore one's own techniques, and find whatever helps. That is the process of the meditation. You cannot over-meditate. Loving-kindness is always appropriate. It is not a disadvantage in the world.

The Buddha lists eleven benefits from the practice of loving-kindness. We will close this meditation by giving the entire discourse. In speaking to the monks, he said,

> O monks, there are eleven benefits from loving-kindness that arise from the emancipation of the heart.
>
> If repeated, developed, made much of, made a habit of, made a basis of, experienced, practiced, well-started, these eleven benefits are expected:
>
> One sleeps well;
> One wakes up well;
> One does not have nightmares;
> One becomes affectionate to human beings;
> One becomes affectionate to non-human beings;
> The deities protect one;
> Neither fire nor poison nor weapons harm one;
> One's mind is easily calmed;
> One's countenance is serene;
> One dies without confusion;
>
> Beyond that, if one fails to attain Nibbana, one is reborn in the higher heavens.

Without a doubt, these are benefits to be earnestly hoped for in one's life. We can see that loving-kindness is not something to be occasionally reflected upon, but "repeated, developed, made much of, made a habit of, and practiced," in order that it does have these benefits.

If it is a fragmentary practice, it will have fragmentary results. If it is a practice deeply steeped into the bones, then it will have a deep and profound result. It is a protection for yourself and a protection for others, both to body and mind. It is conducive to a great stability and sanity. It ensures one's maximum enjoyment of this life and pre-disposes one to an optimal fate after death.

So I leave you with these words and images from the Buddha on the practice of loving-kindness or profound friendliness. May you be well, happy, and peaceful.

Birken Forest Monastery
www.birken.ca
(Transcription by Donna Woods)

Now, we will apply Ajahn Sona's instructions. If you go on retreats, loving kindness is a familiar practice. You can make your own CD of my guided meditation below. If you read it slowly with appropriate pauses it should take about 15 minutes. You can play it back for yourself when you meditate. The advantage of following a guided meditation is that it's easier to do than trying to remember all the ways to develop and direct loving kindness. It's like your mother reading you a bedtime story. You just follow along and accept the suggestions so there's less effort needed. You're encouraged to experiment with it, change it and use personalized images that work for you.

The Guided Meditation on Loving Kindness

Sit upright in meditation posture and close your eyes. Begin with thoughts of friendliness... warmth, loving kindness... then direct that feeling of loving kindness to yourself. Overspread yourself with that friendliness, thinking, "May I be happy. May I find true happiness." And realize the rightness of your wish to be happy. And where does true happiness come from? It has to come from within. And the more happiness you have, the more you naturally share with others, thinking, "May I be happy. May I find true happiness." And smile to invoke that feeling of happiness. Then bring your attention to your heart — your heart centre and dissolve away any ill-will towards yourself. You realize that you have goodness and gentleness in you already. You don't have to be hard on yourself. And you chant to yourself... "May I be well, happy and peaceful. May I be well, happy and peaceful... May I be free from affliction, free from anxiety, free from hostility. May I be well..." And you can visualize yourself sitting in a hot tub, filled to your chin with this white, warm, luminous loving kindness, friendliness, dissolving away your anger and your tension. And it's saturating your body and your mind. Imagine yourself floating in this tranquil space, feeling the best you've ever felt. You can recall memories from your life of times when people were tremendously kind towards you. Or think of moments when you were very kind to others, and get that feeling. You can alter and exaggerate those images to enhance that feeling of metta. Metta means a deep profound friendliness towards yourself and others. It is the emotion and nothing other than the emotion that is loving kindness, not the words. And you can use images from fiction, like novels or movies that inspire feelings of upliftedness or friendliness. You can even use poetry or songs — whatever works for you. Thinking, "May I be happy. May I find true happiness!" Next, extend that feeling of friendliness outwards to a dearly loved friend or family member, wishing, "May they be happy! May they find true happiness as well!" And imagine them sitting right in front of you and you're feeling their presence here. From your heart centre you're enveloping them with your feelings of love and gratitude. Then imagine that they are sending loving kindness to you. And you're exchanging that feeling back and forth. You build that feeling of metta on the friend. Next, think of a benefactor... someone who has helped you a lot in your life, such as a parent or a teacher and visualize them bathed in sunshine, smiling, happy and extend loving kindness to them in the same way, wishing, "May they be happy. May they find true happiness."

Then send loving kindness to your family and friends, those closest to you. You could visualize them all in the same way, bathed in sunshine, smiling, happy. Then send loving kindness to more neutral persons, colleagues, teachers, students, neighbours, acquaintances, strangers, people you meet in shops. Give your loving kindness to everyone without thought of your relationship to them. Then, think of someone you're having difficulties with but think of them as a stranger in a crowd of people and extend your feeling to them as though they were a neutral person. Try to neutralize any feeling of aversion, thinking,

"May they be peaceful, may they be at ease." See if you can extend some loving kindness to them, to break down these barriers in your own heart.

Next, extend your loving kindness to everyone in the room, in the building, then spread it around the neighbourhood north and south, east and west, like a blanket of loving kindness a mile thick covering the whole city, saturating all sentient beings with this friendliness and love. And you can chant to yourself, "May all beings be well, happy and peaceful. May all beings be well, happy and peaceful." In the Metta sutta the Buddha said:

> Wishing, in gladness and in safety,
> May all beings be at ease!
> Whatever living beings there may be;
> Whether they are weak or strong, omitting none,
> The great or the mighty, medium, short or small,
> The seen and the unseen,
> Those living near and far away,
> Those born and to-be-born
> May all beings be at ease!
> Let none deceive another,
> Or despise any being in any state.
> Let none through anger or ill-will
> Wish harm upon another.
> Even as a mother protects with her life
> Her child, her only child,
> So with a boundless heart
> Should one cherish all living beings;
> Radiating kindness over the entire world:
> Spreading upwards to the skies,
> And downwards to the depths;
> Outwards and unbounded,
> Freed from hatred and ill-will.

Whether standing or walking, seated or lying down
Free from drowsiness,
One should sustain this recollection...

This is said to be the sublime abiding corresponding to the heavenly state but heaven happens from you not to you. It is by generating and developing loving kindness in your mind and in your heart that you can create this heavenly condition in your life. So, expand that feeling further across the whole province, the whole country and the continent and expand it out over the entire world wishing, "May all beings be well, happy and peaceful. May all beings be well, happy and peaceful."

Then... send that loving kindness up into the sky, to the beings that live in the sky, and to the higher realms of existence, the devas, the heavenly beings. Tune into their happiness in their celestial palaces and visualize that as you are sending loving kindness upwards to them, in response, they're sending their loving kindness down here to you like a funnel of love saturating the space here with the luminosity of their loving kindness and benevolence and you feel their presence and their intelligence and their power. You're breathing in the luminosity of their loving kindness and it's saturating your body and your mind and you're chanting "May all devas be well, happy and peaceful. May all devas be well happy and peaceful."

Later, send your loving kindness below you into the earth, to the beings that live in the earth and to the lower realms of existence — the animal realm and the ghost realm. Give your warmth and friendliness to them as well. And then bring it up and extend your loving kindness around and across and everywhere. Imagine waves and waves of loving kindness emanating from your heart centre across the world. Then, bring that loving kindness back to yourself. Fill yourself like a vessel, filled to the top with that white warm luminous friendliness, loving kindness, thinking, "May I be happy. May I find true happiness!" Then dissolve the contemplation and open your eyes.

Commentary

The loving kindness is a real touchy-feely practice. It's nice and enjoyable to do. It's easier than the breath because the breath is a non-conceptual practice. There's no concept. You're just meditating on the sensation of the breath touching your skin. It's a body meditation actually, but the loving kindness is a conceptual practice. You're contemplating upon the theme of profound friendliness. You're focusing your attention onto that area of your mind and expanding it outwards so that it pervades your being. The opposite of that is when you focus in on who you resent and expand that outwards until you feel like picking up the phone and telling them off. This shows the karma of sustained thought. If you have that sustained thought of goodwill and love, that is a karmic event because karma works through body, speech and mind. If you say something or do something, that is karma, but at the level of thought, even if you don't say or do anything, if you have that sustained intention of metta then it's a wholesome karmic act which will come back to you in a beneficial way. The Buddha was very concerned that the opposite is true. A sustained thought of ill-will, anger, resentment is negative karma that will rebound upon you in the future. Therefore, this practice of metta is a karmically very significant practice. If you keep it up for years you can become the kind of person that everybody likes to be around — beaming with friendliness, confidence and cheerfulness. Metta dissolves your aversion at a deep level like a solvent and in my own experience it has given me the power to be able to shift my thoughts when I get a bit depressed or negative. Since the time I first went to the Birken Forest Monastery in 2001, I've made metta my main meditation practice because of how skilfully Ajahn Sona taught it. You can listen to several of his discourses on loving kindness on the Birken website. He told me "You can make a whole life out of loving kindness."

During walking meditation you can practice loving kindness. As you walk down the path visualize the person you are sending loving kindness to, at the end of the path, thinking "May you be well, happy and peaceful." When you turn around, see them at the other end of the path, or imagine the next person you want to send metta to. Be creative. You can even imagine giving each other a hug when you get to the end of the path. Loving kindness can also be done as a lying meditation. It's a gentle way of getting up in the morning instead of just hauling your butt out of bed right away. You wish that all beings be happy, be safe.

You can kick start your metta practice by imagining that you're holding, close to your face, an object that makes the mind melt, like a cat or a puppy or a baby, wishing "May it be well, happy and peaceful." After you build up that feeling, merge that image into your own heart, your heart centre and extend loving kindness to yourself. That's the technique for people who have self hate. If they feel that they can't send metta to themselves they can do this first, or send it to someone that they admire because even people who hate themselves admire somebody. Once they genuinely feel some love, then that's the time to try to pour some of that feeling on themselves. I explained this to a woman in one of my classes and then she burst into tears saying that she did have self hate and this is just what she needed to hear.

One of the methods of practicing metta is to visualize a curtain with a being behind that curtain. You don't know who or what the being is but you are sending loving kindness to them anyway. Then imagine the curtain opening and you see who is there. You can let your mind spontaneously come up with a being or you can choose one after you've sent metta to them. Play with it. The curtain opens and you could see your mother standing there, or your brother or your friend. Then they walk away and the curtain closes again and now there's another being there that you can't see. You send them loving kindness and the curtain opens and it's President Barak Obama, then a total stranger, then a cat, a dog, then a difficult person. It could be Adolf Hitler. Keep experimenting with all sorts of people and beings. Eventually it helps to give you a feeling of anatta, non self. It doesn't matter who or what is there, you're sending loving kindness to all beings without distinction.

There's a story from Buddhaghosa, though it's not in the suttas, that the Buddha taught this metta practice to a group of monks. The monks were being tormented by devas who were trying to drive them out of their home region because they had overstayed their welcome. The devas created fearful appearances and foul smelling odors. The monks got up, all at once, and left and went to the Buddha to ask for a better retreat location. The Buddha said, "No. You must go back to that place." "But what about those fearful apparitions and the foul odors?!" the monks protested. "Before you were without weapons", the Buddha taught. "Now, I will give you the weapons of loving kindness." So he taught them the metta practice and they went back and their retreat was very successful; the devas loved the monks, and in return they made their rains retreat very pleasant by making food appear and by conducting them to their kutis to meditate.

The antidote to anger or aversion is to contemplate upon it's wholesome opposite, friendliness. This is a very wholesome meditation practice and it works indirectly. If you are angry at someone you counteract that by sending loving-kindness to yourself first, then to a very dearly loved friend and then to neutral people. After you have genuinely built up some feeling of friendliness, benevolence and love towards yourself, the friend and a neutral person, then you try to think of the hostile person as a neutral person. This is a skillful way of sending loving-kindness to difficult people.

Some people think that if they are angry at someone they should send them loving kindness, but that's not always good advice. Someone may feel worse about themselves if they attempt but fail in the attempt, feeling that they are incapable of generating kindness. If you use the indirect approach, what matters is that you are displacing the ill-will and aversion in your mind with friendliness

A Short Walk On An Ancient Path

by sending it to yourself and to a dearly loved friend or benefactor. That's great, just to go that far. You can stop there if you want, with the anger quelled. You don't have to send it to the difficult person.

U Silananda teaches that "When doing the metta chant, "May all beings...," three to ten times should be standard. When we send these metta thoughts, we can send them in different ways; we can send them by location or by persons. When we say the sentences, we should try to visualize the beings or persons mentioned in the sentences as being really happy and peaceful"(Paritta Pali, 1995; 70).

It is necessary to love yourself first, the Buddha taught, in order to be able to extend true loving kindness to others. Love everyone unconditionally — including yourself. The people with the most love and compassion in the world are the arahants; that's why we think of them.

In the *Path of Purification,* Buddhaghosa writes (Nanamoli, 1956; 323):

[If one develops their loving kindness contemplation] in this way 'I am happy. Just as I want to be happy and dread pain, as I want to live and not to die, so do other beings, too,' making himself the example, then desire for other beings' welfare and happiness arises in him. And this method is indicated by the Blessed One's saying.

> *I visited all quarters with my mind*
> *Nor found I any dearer than myself;*
> *Self is likewise to every other dear;*
> *Who loves himself will never harm another.*
> *(S.i, 75; Ud. 47)*

So he should first, as example, pervade himself with lovingkindness. Next after that, in order to proceed easily, he can recollect such gifts, kind words, etc., as inspire love and endearment, such virtue, learning, etc., as inspire respect and reverence met with in a teacher or his equivalent or a preceptor or his equivalent, developing lovingkindness towards him in the way beginning 'May this good man be happy and free from suffering.' With such a person, of course, he attains absorption.

But if this bhikkhu does not rest content with just that much and wants to break down the barriers, he should next after that, develop lovingkindness towards a very dearly loved friend, then towards a neutral person as a very dearly loved friend, then towards a hostile person as neutral. And while he does so, he should make his mind malleable and wieldy in each instance before passing on to the next."

Buddhaghosa continues with nineteen pages of commentary on this loving kindness practice, which is recommended reading. The benefits of loving-kindness are to be aspired towards but it takes regular practice which should be repeated, developed, made much of and made a habit of, in order that it does uplift your life. It leads to great strength and happiness in one's mind. The fruition of loving kindness is playfulness.

You can follow my guided meditation CD with tracks 5 and 6, which is a 10-minute guided contemplation on loving-kindness followed by a 20-minute guided contemplation on loving-kindness. You can do the short one or you can really bliss out and do a whole half hour in a row if you like. The short guided meditation is also freely available on my website at theravada.ca .

Walking Meditation

Walking meditation compliments sitting meditation. This keeps you awake, stretches the legs and it is a transition to the post meditation world. You can walk for the same period of time or a shorter length. You can do the walking first to settle yourself down, then go straight into sitting without a break. To do this, as in sitting meditation it is important to have direct personal instruction. You can put your hands together in front or behind you to prevent them from swinging and people seem to concentrate better with their hands together. Don't clasp too tight. Relax into it.

You concentrate on your feet — the object of meditation. You don't need to meditate on the breath because that's too subtle a sensation. If you need to save space in a group you can walk in a clockwise circle. When people greeted the Buddha they kept their right side to the Buddha in coming or going. So when you go clockwise, you are keeping your right side to the centre. Many people say that they like walking meditation more than sitting because it gives them something to do; it keeps them in their body. When they sit they just space out and their mind is all over the place. On other days they will say that walking meditation is more distracting than sitting because they're moving around and their eyes are open. It's good to practice either technique depending upon what's right for you. Walking meditation stretches the legs and wakes you up if you have done a lot of sitting. The dictionary definition of the word "step" is: "An act of progressive motion that requires one of the supporting limbs of the body to be thrust in the direction of the movement, and to reassume its function of support; a pace." But, you're not supposed to be thinking about that when you step; just step.

Walking keeps people awake. Many of my students report that their sitting gets more concentrated after the walking meditation. This is because the walking builds up your concentration, then you go right into the sitting without a break. This is why Ajahn Supan taught me, when I was a monk, to do the walking meditation first and then the sitting. Below are instructions from Ajahn Kusalo at www.BuddhaMind.info.

Walking meditation has many facets; it can be considered simply as an alternative posture. Unless you are very lucky, sitting for more than an hour or so is quite physically difficult — there is a need to unravel the bones and muscles. Yoga and tai chi are good for this but walking is an easily developed technique which can maintain the direct thread of one's meditation. If you can give the time, extended periods of formal meditation are usually very fruitful and when you do change posture it is good to reflect on how the mind shifts with that change. There is a tendency to divide meditation into sitting and, 'all the rest.' The encouragement is to maintain mindfulness in all four postures; sitting, standing, walking and lying down. This does take quite some practice and the use of structured exercises is very supportive in establishing a strong internal sense of just what mindfulness is.

Boundaries:

As with any meditation technique it is important to set up boundaries. The overall idea being to determine an object of meditation for a determined amount of time. With breath meditation one might say: 'Now I determine to watch the breath for 40 minutes.' With walking meditation the path one selects creates the boundary. One chooses a stretch of (relatively) level ground — about 20 to 30 paces long — and marks either end in some way. This can be with sticks or rocks or piles of leaves — anything will do as long as it is quite clear. Between two trees is a traditional path but these are not readily come by so well placed. If you find walking useful and think to do a lot then you can build a path with brick edging and gravel or bark floor — or whatever materials you have to hand. The advantage the boundaries of a walking path have over say those of breath meditation is that they are much more tangible. If you were walking between two trees you would be conveniently reminded that you had lost mindfulness when you got to the end of the path and bent your nose against the tree.

Walk on:

The defined nature of a path helps contain the mind and the tendency to wander. Begin at one end of the path. Bring attention to the body. You could spend a few moments doing 'body sweeping'. Feel a sense of balance — both internal and external. Determine for how long you will walk. Let go of expectations. Relax. The usual suggestion is to maintain the focus on the feelings at the soles of the feet — this helps define the boundary further. There is the possibility of distraction, and one can get caught in looking at the clouds or the flowers or the birds, etc.. Walk with eyes downcast, looking about three paces ahead. Proceed at a 'normal' pace. Get to the end of the path — stop — turn around — stop — begin walking. Try this for at least 15 minutes. An hour is good too.

Variants:

You can experiment with the point of focus. The swing of the arms — or just the hands. The balance of the head (as in walking with a book on top of). Try keeping attention on the sensation of 'the whole body walking'. Or, the sensations of the wind or the sun on the body. Or joining

A Short Walk On An Ancient Path

walking with breath meditation. Try walking very slowly, noting each shift of the body, the positions of the feet and legs. You could formularise this: lifting left leg, stepping forward, reaching, lowering, placing, transferring weight, etc. If you are limited by space — especially if you are indoors — you could try circumambulating a room. You could do this with a group of people — there is no leader and a need to be sensitive to the group energy/speed. You could combine walking with chanting (it is fairly common for monastics to learn their chanting on the walking path). Try noting the beginning, middle and end of each length of the path (as with the breath). Note the intention to stop (easy, as it is signed by the end of the path); the intention to turn around (not so easy as it is only signed by a movement of the mind). It is good to develop personal boundaries or a style and just work with that. Be careful of the butterfly practice — 5 minutes of this, a bit of the other, etc. Be clear that you are being clear.

Generally:

- Set your session up with the attitude of having nothing to get and, literally, nowhere to go. You can just enjoy a walk. Relax.

- Adjust the pace to suit your state of mind. Walk vigorously when drowsy or trapped in obsessive thought — like worry, anger, fear. If you are restless or impatient maintain a firm, gentle and steady pace. Get a sense of your internal energy and then set a pace to balance that.

- Walking can be an occasion for insight. As a good portion of the thinkery is involved in keeping the body upright and forwarding, thought tends to be reduced and the mind can shift into 'neutral' quite easily. It is often into this 'doing nothing', letting it be' space that insight will arise.

- Associate your walking practice with 'every day' walking. Bring the sense of composure, containment, focus, etc. into your mind as you walk from your bedroom into the kitchen — down the road — in the shops (especially the eyes downcast part). This will greatly support your mindfulness in 'the world'.

Lying down:

- As one of the four postures this can be used for meditation. Lie full length on your (right) side with the left arm laying along your upper side and the right arm under your head (or vice versa). One can relax the body but there is a sense of being balanced on one side which helps stop one from falling asleep.

- A common thing is not having enough time to meditate. You could try bed time meditation. At the end of the day — you have switched the light out — it is time for sleep. Usually there is some time before you actually fall asleep. Use this time for meditation. Relax. Breathe. Silently recite a mantra. Practice metta. You can develop a range of practices. This will make falling asleep easier and will affect the quality both of your sleep and your waking.

- If you do keep falling asleep during your meditation time perhaps you just need some sleep. It is not uncommon that people's energy is dependent on external stimulus. The first days of a meditation retreat — without that stimulus — and they are falling asleep all over the place. Make an effort but be compassionate.

To expand upon the lying meditation, in lying meditation you do much the same as in sitting meditation. You lie down, preferably on your right side, the Buddha taught, because your heart is on the left side. It puts less pressure on your heart. You can do breath or loving kindness practice the same way as with sitting. It's also great to do if you can't sleep in the middle of the night. For people who say that they don't have enough time to meditate, this is the time! No excuse. It's 4:00 am and you can't sleep. You don't want to disturb your partner by reading, even with an itty bitty book light, so practice meditation to cut through that insomnia. Often people are awake because they are worrying about their job or relationship or whatever, so you can cut through that neurosis and those thoughts going around and around by meditating until you fall back asleep. This makes the mind more peaceful and helps you to sleep and it's better than counting sheep. The Buddha said that a monk or nun should be mindful until the last moment of consciousness, and then immediately resume mindfulness practice as soon as they wake up. You shouldn't lie down if you want to meditate because you'll likely fall asleep. The rule is, if you want to meditate then sit; if you are lying down, then meditate. Lying meditation is meant for situations where you are lying down anyhow, like going to bed, or when you're sick. This is good for cold winters when you don't want to get out of your cozy bed, snuggled up to another warm lovable body beside you. It also a good time to practice metta. When you wake up you don't have to haul yourself out of bed straight away. You can gently start the day thinking "May I be happy. May all beings be well, happy and peaceful." I do lying meditation almost every night.

Ordinary Walking

When walking down the street you shouldn't use the usual walking meditation technique. You are moving faster and you need to be on the lookout for cars and people but you can still practice mindfulness. Usually our minds are all over the place when we're walking around in the city and we don't pay much attention to sensations in the body. You can still note the feet touching the ground. Bring your attention to your right foot as it touches the pavement. You say to yourself "Right, left, right, right, right. Right, left, right, right, right," as you walk along. You skip most of the left counts, otherwise you would be noting too fast for comfort. You can still practice mindfulness/ awareness in this way, in the midst of noisy traffic. We walk so often, even close to home so this is a true opportunity to practice dhamma.

Standing Meditation

There are four postures for meditation practice — sitting, walking, standing and lying. Ananda confused the arahant policy by attaining enlightenment in another posture. He was trying hard to get to nirvana. A few weeks after the Buddha died he took a break from his meditation. He was on the verge of assuming his laying down position when just as his hand touched the mat, pop! He attained full and permanent enlightenment.

To do standing meditation you stand with your hands comfortably at your side or together. Your balance is better with your eyes open. Cast your eyes down, in front of you. You can do a similar technique of breath or metta meditation as you do in sitting practice. With your eyes open you still follow the breath but you can put more attention on the sensations of standing. Scan your body up and down practicing mindfulness of the body. It's natural to do this when you're doing walking meditation. When you turn around, just stop and pause and stand. Sometimes if your mind races ahead of you when walking, it's good to stop and do standing meditation to let it catch up. It's like when you're with a small child that races ahead of you and you fold your arms and stop, saying "Come back! I'm not moving until you come back! I'm going to stay right here."

This is a good technique if you've been meditating too long and need to stand up. This overcomes sleepiness. For a group in a crowded room with no space for walking meditation, use standing instead. This is a great one for line ups too, line ups anywhere, or bus stops because you don't look weird with your hands hanging at your side. Let such mindfulness practices infiltrate your being. Build a lifestyle of mindfulness. It is by being so ordinary that life takes on an extraordinary quality. Simplifying your life is defined as creating an environment in your life that allows you to be more mindful. When I was 20 my buddy from high school and I drove from Ontario to move to Vancouver and we visited my sister Diana. I was telling her about living "here and now". She thought I was talking irresponsibly about 'eat, drink and be merry' and we left without me really being able to express myself correctly. Thirteen years later when I was living in the monastery in Thailand I finally understood what being here and now meant. After three weeks of a retreat the mindfulness sunk into me at an experiential level. With mindfulness life can take on a 'sparkle in the rain' quality.

Going into the Silence

The technique of going into the silence is for allowing answers to spring forth which may be buried under your confusion or in your subconscious mind. You must listen to the still small voice within. If an answer is coming, it will come from that still small voice within you. Do not practice conventional meditation but sit, wide awake with your eyes open and do nothing. You can write down the question you are asking or what the issue is and try to be as clear as you can. You do not try to figure out an answer. When your mind wanders, gently bring it back to the question. You remain open and wait for 30 minutes, 40 minutes. After this you may notice a stream of thoughts starting to flow through you. Sometimes, after a whole hour, 'bang!' an answer will pop into your mind that is complete and satisfying, clear and meaningful to you. Usually it is accompanied by the energy to immediately act on it. You may even have to go to the bathroom. This method works simply by creating a container around your mind in this way. This allows the fragile connection within to be nurtured. In our society it is rare for someone to sit attentively for an hour and do absolutely nothing. Our work ethic always keeps us busy. But, there is no faster way to get an answer to a question. I urge you to try it. I give credit to Brian Tracy for these "going into the silence" teachings.

The Four Foundations of Mindfulness

"If you have time to be mindful, you have time to meditate."
Ajahn Chah

Meditation is practiced from the perspective of what the Buddha called the four foundations of mindfulness.
1. Mindfulness of body — body position and movement.
2. Mindfulness of feelings — pleasant, unpleasant and neutral feelings.
3. Mindfulness of mind — awareness itself, as well as your underlying state of mind — expanded or contracted, etc.

4. Mindfulness of mind objects and dhamma categories — the six senses — thinking, seeing, hearing, feeling, smell and taste as well as the five hindrances, etc.

Every experience that you have had can be found under one of these four categories. Mindfulness of the body is the best place to start, the first aggregate of form. In meditation you are aware when your body acts up and distracts you. In post meditation you should make an effort to be mindful in each waking minute. That means that you should focus your mind on what it is that you are actually doing or contemplating. You can practice this with mindful eating. Some people say that this is almost a revelation to them, they realize that they were missing moments of their life. The discipline is to stop reading the newspaper (it's mostly negative anyway) while you eat, and stop listening to the radio at the same time. Just eat. This is meditation in action, you regard your eating and other activities as an extension of your sitting practice. When you meditate you don't read the newspaper and listen to music.

In reaching for a spoonful of cereal you can be silently mindful or you can use the noting technique, saying to yourself "reaching." You can note each part of the movement and mindfully eat the whole meal that way. You don't have to go particularly slow. The Buddha never associated mindfulness with moving slowly and he didn't act in a strange way. He ate his food the same as everyone else. You can continue to be aware of "chewing, chewing, tasting, tasting," noting "liking," or "disliking." "Swallowing, swallowing," as you feel it going down the throat. Meals in silence are a wonderful practice experience in family life. You don't have to have every meal in silence but it would be wise to do so at the right time. Phra Sawat, my meditation instructor at Wat Ram Poeng used to walk past me and my compadres many times saying only "Acknowledge, acknowledge."

The second foundation of mindfulness, mindfulness of feelings means that you catch yourself whenever your mind adversely turns away from things that bug you in the slightest way, plus note things that tempt your attention, and also note things that are neither pleasant, nor unpleasant — neutral feelings. This is a completely different meaning for 'feelings' than the 'feeling' in the 2nd aggregate of anatta (which means the five senses).

To remember the third and fourth foundations, there is an image which helps to anchor these concepts. It is of a goldfish swimming around in a goldfish bowl. The fourth foundation is represented by the bright goldfish. The mind objects are the bright reflections off the fins and body which are easy to see. What is not so easy to see and appreciate is the water around the goldfish. This is the mind itself, and the underlying state of mind (how clean the water is). Is your underlying state of mind joyous, rapturous, depressed, confused? All of your thoughts and sensory input from seeing hearing, etc. are mind objects, which are very dominating in your experience, practically the whole of your experience. Behind it all, your awareness is there, consciousness itself.

A Buddha statue at the Birken Forest Monastery

Golden stupa at the Grand Palace, Bangkok

Chapter 3

The Eightfold Path

*"That's one small step for a man,
one giant leap for mankind!"*

Have you heard of the new Buddhist email filter? It doesn't allow any attachments.

I recommend reading the clear and succinct book, *The Noble Eightfold Path* by Bhikkhu Bodhi. The eightfold path is the fourth noble truth. This is the truth that there is a way out of suffering; there is a way out of here. The Buddha prescribed his teaching like a doctor for the world, and he said that the way to reach the deathless state of nirvana is by practising eight things. Sometimes we experience moments of peace, moments of tranquility, but we cannot sustain that for very long. Even if we stop our thoughts and rest the mind in the deep bliss of jhana, we can't keep it up for long. We need some kind of discipline to bring us to letting be. We need to walk on a spiritual path of some kind. This is the great pilgrimage from here to here.

First, an overview of the path, then more detail on each one. This approach comes from a time management philosophy about how to read a book, which is taught by Brian Tracy. People retain information better if they first look over a book and read the table of contents. Then read the first line or so of each chapter. Next, randomly skim through the book to get a feel for how the book is laid out. After this approach, you go back and read the whole book from page one. This gives your mind a conceptual framework for which to plug in information from the book, so your memory retention is better. Let this guide your Buddhist learning methods. This has an affect on how I teach Buddhism. The overview of the path to nirvana is traditionally depicted by a wheel with eight spokes.

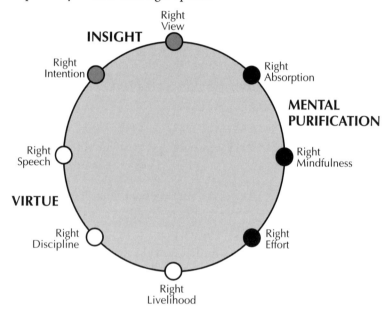

The eight are divided into three inseparable stages:
> **Virtue:** right speech, right discipline, right livelihood.
> **Mental purification:** right effort, right mindfulness, right absorption.
> **Insight or wisdom:** right view, right intention.

The Buddha taught this path in his first discourse. Of great historic significance, the Buddha first turned the wheel of his teachings in Deer Park for his five former colleagues. This path is called "the middle way," meaning, the avoidance of extremes. Avoid the extreme of indulgence in sensuous pleasure which is 'painful, unworthy and unprofitable,' and avoid the extreme of self mortification with asceticism. As shown, the path is divided into three stages: virtue, mental purification, insight. In Pali, the original terms for these three are sila, samadhi and pannya. As much as possible in this book an effort is made to try to use plain English, but there are some terms from Pali which should be explained. Morality, ethical conduct, is based upon the Buddha's vast conception of universal love and compassion for all living beings. This basis of the Buddhist path is not a dry set of rules. The Buddha gave his teaching with heart 'for the good of the many, for the happiness of the many, out of compassion for the world.' In order to be perfect a person must develop equally the two qualities of compassion and wisdom.

It would be a mistake to think of the eightfold Path as a highway to nirvana where you just set the cruise control and then sit back. The Buddha used the word 'magga' which means path but it is like the foot prints left by an animal. It's tricky to find, like with a farmer looking for a lost cow. He sees the footprints on the ground but then it goes across gravel and rocks. It's very difficult to tell where the beast has been. So even at the best of times, when you have an excellent teacher to personally guide you, it's easy to get side tracked off the eightfold Path. These eight parts of the path are to be practiced concurrently as a way of life. They are not steps so much as components of a whole, like strands of a cable. Here are each of the 'Rights.'

Right View

The first step along the path is right view. The seven other points pivot around the first one. Right view is like a detailed map that clearly explains the way. Once you know the way you don't need to read the map. Experience is always better than going by a book. You should develop a precise view about the nature of the four noble truths, a precise view of the eightfold path and a precise view of the nature of the mind. In one of the suttas the Buddha said "Right view is karma and rebirth." Ajahn Sona teaches that "karma and rebirth is the overarching ultimate view of reality in Buddhism." It is such an important and far reaching teaching of the Buddha that Chapter 4 is devoted to this. The Buddha was very clear in defining what he meant by right view. One attained to right view would see the world as follows: "He has right view, undistorted vision, thus: 'There is that which is given and what is offered and what is sacrificed; there is fruit and result of good and bad actions; there is this world and the other world; there is mother and father; there are beings who are reborn spontaneously; there are good and virtuous recluses and brahmins in the world who have themselves realized by direct knowledge and declare this world and the other world'" (*Majjhima Nikaya* 41.14).

The view also includes non self and non theism. It means to study the dharma, to wisely reflect upon the teachings. The Buddha taught that wise reflection is the most important inner quality. The most important outer quality is the kalyanamitra — the spiritual friend. If you just use one meditation technique then, as Ajahn Geoff says, it's like trying to build a house with just a hammer. Without wise reflection you keep grinding away with Vipassana meditation or whatever it is, but you are well advised to learn more techniques. Meditation is not enough. Meditation is number six, seven and eight on the path. If you only meditate without balancing that with study, then there is a danger that your meditation practise will become self oriented or that you will be an 'ignorant meditator.' It takes study and contemplation to penetrate right view. The Buddha said that what he had to teach was difficult to understand, comprehensible only to the wise. We must always be trying to clarify our view and refine our understanding. By discussing our view with teachers we can quickly clarify our assumptions. It saves you a lot of time by humbling yourself and opening yourself to correction.

It is wrong view to say that it's best to have no view at all. The Pali word 'ditupadona' is explained as the 'clinging to wrong views.' This gets misconstrued and people think that clinging to any view is wrong. Being 'possessed of right view' is a tangible thing — it's clear, not fuzzy.

The Very Venerable Ajahn Brahm in Perth, said, "A common wrong view is the idea that all religions are paths to a mountaintop. This is not what the Buddha taught. Whatever religion or philosophy or teachings which practices the eightfold path and produces stream enterers, once returners, non returners and arahants, can be taken as the teachings of the Buddha," he said.

The view of the mind is that it has no permanent identity; it is without a separate independent self. Your mind is not a personal thing. If you go and look for your mind, you cannot find it. Where is your mind? That is the view. Wrong view is like starting your car and pulling off the curb, without knowing how to drive. In the Net of Views discourse, the Brahmajala sutta, the Buddha listed 62 wrong views which encompass every other religion in the world. Just as a fish jumps out of a net in the water, the Buddha said, the fish just falls right back into the net again.

Right Intention

In, *The Noble Eightfold Path,* Bhikkhu Bodhi writes, "The Buddha explains right intention as threefold: the intention of renunciation, the intention of good will, and the intention of harmlessness" (Bodhi, 1994; 29). The intention of non ill-will or harmlessness could mean stillness, equanimity; it doesn't have to mean loving kindness. The point is to get rid of the feeling of ill-will. Renunciation means the letting go of things; it counteracts unwholesome desire. The first two parts of the path, view and intention, comprise the insight stage of the path — pannya, wisdom. It is noteworthy that the highest wisdom in Buddhist philosophy is associated with the view and intention of love and compassion. These noblest of qualities are placed at the highest stage of the path. Having wisdom means having love, compassion, virtue and the aspiration to help others. This love and truth should not be lost in an analysis of what Buddhist mind training is all about. Knowing the view is not enough. Right intention implies the choice to follow that path of awakening.

Right Speech

"Any speech which ignores uncertainty is not the speech of a sage."
Ajahn Chah

The virtue stage is described in the next three parts of the eightfold path. These ethical guidelines restrain immoral actions but their deeper purpose is not moral as much as spiritual. Ultimately they are the foundation for mental purification. If you live ethically your meditation practice is not disturbed by thoughts of remorse and worry. The first of the next three parts is right speech. The Buddha taught that there are three gates by which you relate with the world — your body, speech and mind. There's an old saying in my country that says "sticks and stones may break my bones, but names will never hurt me," but don't believe it. Words can start wars and get people killed, or heal divisions between people and bring peace. It is very important to watch over your gate of speech. Right speech means to speak concisely, with as few words as necessary. Speak if it will improve upon silence. The Buddha said that when his disciples meet they should do either of two things: discuss the dharma, or maintain noble silence. Mr. Spock in Star Trek may have been modeled after the Buddhist ideal of right speech. Gene Roddenberry, the creator of Star Trek was influenced by Buddhism. Mr. Spock spoke concisely and with such presence, that his character won a cult following, which was unexpected by NBC. Role models are a good thing for you to use for any area of your life, so you can use Spock as well as the Buddha, if you like.

The Sanskrit word 'vac' translates as 'speech' and it also means 'utterance,' 'word,' 'logos.' It implies perfect communication, the direct approach. For example, you say "The great white north is cold." You do not say "I think that the great white north is sort of cold 'round abouts this time of year." Being direct, you just say "It is so." "Fire is hot." "Shit happens." Such communication is true speech. However, this does not deny the value of being indirect in social situations when you need to express something in a polite way. Honesty is also included in right speech. One should avoid lying, avoid useless babble, idle chit chat, gossip, backbiting, or slander. Don't use words or tones that are divisive, malicious, harsh, abusive, impolite, rude, or angry. The Buddha also pointed out that speech should be timely, not untimely. If you plan to bring up a certain point at a meeting and you get a strong feeling there, that you shouldn't talk about it, then listen to your feelings and don't say it! Timing is everything. If you clean up your speech, your words will become truthful and more benevolent and friendly, pleasant and gentle, meaningful and useful. People will stop tuning you out, your every word will have weight. Nobody listens to someone who never stops talking. Your words can become like music to others; you walk into a room and everyone feels upright.

The third precept prescribed by the Buddha is, do not speak falsehoods. That doesn't mean that you have to tell the truth. It means that you shouldn't lie. Speech should be truthful and beneficial. If the truth is not beneficial, then why say it?

The Buddha taught that the four ways of answering a question are:
1. Put the question aside and not answer it.
2. Answer the question directly.
3. Answer the question with another question.
4. Answer the question through analysis.

There are many examples in the suttas of the Buddha refusing to answer questions. Once, an ascetic wanderer asked the Blessed One if there is a self or if there is not a self. The Buddha was silent, so the wanderer wandered away. Later the Buddha explained to Ananda that this particular person would have been even more confused, with even wronger views had the Buddha answered his question. So, he put the question aside.

My own personal opinion about putting the 'do not speak falsehoods' precept into practice is that almost everyone finds it almost impossible. I'm not talking about avoiding malicious lies or conning people out of their money. That is wrong and it can be stopped. But what about when your friend shows up at a party with a hideous new dress and she asks you "Do you like my dress?" If you tell her the truth, you'll hurt her feelings and it's too late for her to go home and change; she's already there. So why hurt her feelings? That's not beneficial. What are you supposed to say? If you have the ability to think on your feet you could put the question aside and not answer it by saying "That's a real change for your wardrobe!" But what if you don't have the ability to think fast on your feet? Is it bad karma for you to lie and say "It's good. It's fine." I don't know. This is the area of white lies which we all face everyday. I guess it's still wrong to tell even a white lie but whatever negative karma there is for telling white lies which are intended to protect people's feelings, it shouldn't be much. We are all very well aware of examples like this from our own social experiences. In April, 1997 the *Vancouver Sun* ran an article right on the front page of the newspaper titled "Most people tell 200 lies each day — honest." In it the reporter says a "psychologist who monitored 20 people says that lying is crucial to functioning society. And life would be a nightmare if we didn't. Analysis of the tapes revealed that an average of one lie was told every eight minutes." "Often, what we are talking about are very small lies, but they are lies none-the-less," said Gerald Jellison, a psychology professor at the University of South California." We find people are almost constantly giving excuses for their failure in behaviour that might be seen by others as inappropriate. A typical comment would be: 'I hate to bother you,' when really they don't give a damn. They will tell lies to relatives or friends on the telephone, perhaps to get out of a dinner. Society would be terrible if people started telling the truth. Anyone who did would be a subversive."

Jellison said the problems of being completely honest are illustrated in the film *Liar Liar.* The film features Jim Carrey as a lawyer, a compulsive liar who reforms and can't stop himself from telling the truth, with alarming results. Other psychologists agree that dishonesty is a fundamental part of life — despite modern-day thinking in favour of openness, and despite the Buddhist precepts. Richard Wiseman, a British psychologist at Hertfordshire University said "Society would

A Short Walk On An Ancient Path

fall apart if we were honest all the time. No one would get a job if they were completely honest on their CV."

In the bigger picture Bhikkhu Bodhi writes (Bodhi, 1994; 49) "It is said that in the course of his long training for enlightenment over many lifetimes, a bodhisatta can break all the moral precepts except the pledge to speak the truth. The reason for this is very profound, and reveals that the commitment to truth has a significance transcending the domain of ethics and even mental purification, taking us to the domains of knowledge and being. Truthful speech provides, in the sphere of interpersonal communication, a parallel to wisdom in the sphere of private understanding." "Devotion to truthful speech is a matter of taking our stand on reality rather than illusion, on the truth grasped by wisdom rather than the fantasies woven by desire."

Right Discipline

Right discipline, morality, or conduct, is number four on the eightfold path. We never have enough self discipline do we? Everybody wants more discipline. Discipline means living within rules. It is discipline that frees you. Putting off discipline imprisons you, like a student that wants to be free of all his work. He slacks off but when exams come he's stressed out. The prepared student breezes through his exams and is free. Discipline is freedom. When I was a monk I had a friend who lived at Phra Payutto's temple outside of Bangkok. Phra Payutto is one of Thailand's most renown scholar monks. I was visiting and my friend, a Swiss monk, told me that the advantage of being in the monkhood was that you cannot do whatever you want. If the community you are living in objects to your natural impulses, then this is a gift of discipline which you can use to tame your mind. The principles of proper moral behaviour, the Buddhist precepts, are the starting point of right discipline. There are 311 precepts for nuns and 227 precepts for monks — each one pronounced by the Buddha himself. The monks robes are like a straight jacket. For lay people, such as ourselves, there are only five precepts.

The Five Precepts

1. Do not kill.
2. Do not take what is not offered.
3. Do not engage in sexual misconduct.
4. Do not speak falsehoods.
5. Do not take alcohol or intoxicants that cloud the mind, because it leads to moral carelessness.

These five precepts prescribed by the Buddha go a long way to promote harmony in society and family. If everyone followed the five precepts we would live in an Utopian world. Can you imagine if nobody lied or ripped people off or killed anybody? This would be a golden age but the Buddha was not God. He gave us the precepts but it's up to us to follow them.

Something must actually be offered before you take it. When I was a kid I sneaked quarters from my mom's purse so I could buy an ice cream sandwich at lunchtime at school, but I was wrong. I should have asked her first, to avoid confusion. Adultery is an obvious form of sexual misconduct. When men or women cheat on their spouse, this can cause turmoil and inner conflict. A man's spouse suffers and she eventually knows about it. If he denies the truth of her feeling this makes her crazy. The other woman suffers too because she secretly hopes that the man will leave his spouse for her. The man suffers from the guilt of his actions and the resultant bad karma. Better to avoid this in the first place by heeding the third precept. The scriptures indicate that sexual misconduct can lead to animal rebirth. One could become an animal having lots and lots of sex with many partners. Oh wonderful. If a man dates a woman but has no intention of being in a relationship with her, and uses her sexually, leading her on, lying, then dumps her, leaving her very hurt, this could be judged as breaking the third precept. Drunk driving deaths are a clear example of the moral carelessness that results from breaking the fifth precept.

Many of the precepts for monks and nuns relate to very limited situations, like deportment or washing their begging bowl. Only about 20 precepts have much of an effect on their behaviour. Adhering to all of the precepts doesn't make one a better person than lay people. One of the precepts made by the Buddha is that a monk or nun cannot sit or lie down suddenly on a bed or a bench with detachable legs, in a loft with an incompletely planked floor, in a dwelling owned by the sangha. Each and every one of these precepts has a particular source story, which caused the Buddha to make each rule. You can just imagine a monk getting bonked on the head by the leg of a bed in the above story, and then the Buddha finding out about it and saying "Oh dear, we had better slap on another precept!" I had to thoroughly study all of the precepts before I ordained as a monk. I thought that it was going to be hundreds of pages of boring reading, but I was pleasantly mistaken. It was only 91 pages (just kidding). In fact, the stories were entertaining, meaningful and gave depth to the social context of the Buddha's time. The precepts and the thousand lesser rules contain sexually explicit literature as well, defining exactly what sex is. It is penetration to the depth of a sesame seed.

Below I transcribed a 1988 talk on Discipline given by the Vajra Regent Osel Tendzin.

In our lives, discipline is the basis of all virtue. All that is good and decent in life arises from discipline. The essence of Buddhism is discipline. And the kernel of discipline is no, the word 'no.' That means no to aggression, no to passion, no to ignorance, no to indulgence of all kinds. It's called the giant NO. A no so big that it's like the sky. No one has ever heard the sound of that no. That's the Buddhist concept of discipline. You have to be a little hard on yourself. You have to say no to yourself. Buddhadharma means not causing harm. The essence is non aggression, that's what makes it dharma, the quality of non aggression. You have to cut your habitual patterns that are anti-dharmic, like snarling at others, substance abuse or overindulgence in sleep. Now, everyone knows what no means, but just in case... no means no. No doesn't mean maybe, it doesn't mean later on, or when no one is looking. No means no. It means saying no to extremes. No to overindulgence. At the core of overindulgence is the idea of 'ME' as a big deal. The 'me' quality permeates everything. It is simply not proper to make a big deal out of one's self- ever. One has to appreciate the all encompassing quality of what 'no' actually means. No means no ego, no ego ever. However, we think that we have time to work this out. But that's more 'me.' There should be more no.

You should be quick to discipline yourself the way you would deal with a child that is in danger. He's playing at the edge of a roof and you say "Stop! Get away from there! Come back!" You wait until later to explain. It doesn't work if you say "You know, you really shouldn't stand there for too long because you might fall off and then your bones could break and your parents would be really upset..." No. You say "Stop! Stop that now!" That's the attitude we should take with regard to our habitual patterns. We can't be too easy with the seductive quality of our passion. The Buddha's right discipline is a feeling of 24 hour involvement with our practise. When our discipline feels continuous we open up to a vaster vision, a profound vision, and we understand the completeness of the Buddha's realization. When we have that connection to our discipline we feel totally connected to the world. Our sitting meditation practice gives us the experience of discipline by solidly sitting, solidly being. We experience the quality of equanimity.

The next part of saying no to ourselves is saying no to anti-dharmic activity. You are more attracted to hearing, contemplating and meditating, than to samsaric activity. This includes gathering the dharmas, to study and ponder upon it; make it a living experience in your life. Then you really feel the path quality altogether. From that appreciation occurs a further realization of your connection to the Buddha. He comes closer in terms of the qualities of the Buddha.

You can't misbehave and say, "Well, I'll start living right tomorrow." Because it's all the same thing. Tomorrow, today, right now. It's all the same. It's like that movie Gone with the Wind, as the house is burning down people rush up to the star and she says, "I'll think about that tomorrow." You can't do that. And you can't be too busy right now to practice discipline. You're not going to be any less busy in the future. The time to practice the dharma is now. There is never going to be another time. Dharma should pervade your life, like dharma, dharma, dharma, a 24 hour experience. You don't want to be into this just half way. None of us do. Buddhism is not the Sunday 'go to meet religion.' It's a way of life.

There is a transition from saying no to yourself and going outwards and working with others. It's hard for us to say no to ourselves but it's very difficult to say no to others. But if you're genuine and truthful, then you must say no. If someone is putting their ego out and laying a trip on others, then it is your duty to say no to that. You can't let them trample on the dharma. By dharma, that means the sanity of existence. If you don't have any compassion for others, or for them, then you won't say no. You'll make excuses, "Well... that's the way things are." That's not the ways things are. The truth is that we all know when bullshit is happening. You can always tell if what you are doing is bullshit by the level of discursiveness involved. You can always tell. And we shouldn't second guess that. Here, discursiveness is something that keeps bugging you in the back of your mind. You feel that you should do something, or you feel that you should stop doing something. Listen to that — that still small voice within.

The benefit, the result of right discipline that manifests in your life is that you have a mind that is expansive, clear, open, and the environment is never clogged up with extraneous discursive qualities.

In *Heart of the Buddha,* Chögyam Trungpa states:

> Right discipline is based upon trust in oneself. The traditional idea of morality is based on a lack of trust in oneself. People have a fear of their aggression and passion, an obsession with their own inadequacies. People who are obsessed with their own inadequacies don't make good Buddhists. The guilt-ridden approach is actually an attempt to confirm one's ego. Trusting in yourself allows you to work skilfully with whatever is happening. Trusting yourself also arouses a sense of trust in others, a sense of heroism, raising the banner of sanity and proclaiming an open way. This vision of good conduct is not dependent on ego.

Right Livelihood

Elite Compassion

Number five on the Buddha's path to awakening is right livelihood. This means to earn your living in a way that does not cause confusion. Almost any occupation will do so long as you acquire your wealth legally, peacefully and honestly. The categories of wrong livelihood are hunting, fishing, dealing in weapons, intoxicants, poisons, slavery of humans, raising animals for slaughter, and butchery. Also, practising deceit, soothsaying, trickery and usury are wrong livelihood. If you work in sales you can provide a product or service which is in accord with right livelihood. You can earn riches. The dharma doesn't denigrate the state of being very wealthy. The Buddha's billionaire benefactor, Anathapindika was the wealthiest supporter of the Buddha and he achieved the saintly status of a stream enterer. The reason why some people may feel that there is something wrong with being wealthy is because Ralph Waldo Emerson said that there is a conspiracy of the vast majority to keep everyone down to an average level of mediocrity. If anyone decides to rise above the crowd and do something special with their life, then there is a flurry of activity in the crowd to keep them back down, so that nobody feels threatened. So consider the possibility that there may be nothing wrong with rich successful people. They may not be unhappy after all, with all their money. They may have more virtue and better karma than ordinary people — that's why their karma resulted in them getting rich. Please let go of the poor monk thing, because we are not monks and nuns.

Right livelihood for a sales person means that if you step across that line and push more onto people than what they want or can use, then you cause confusion. The customer goes home and wonders why he bought so much unnecessary attachments from you. You have stepped into the darkness. But if you sell white toilet paper rolls at a competitive price that saves poor people three cents per roll, then you are benefiting the poor that way. There's no panhandlers that you have to support but it would be even better to use your money to help others. You can expand your business and net $500,000 per year, growing at an average of 10% a year for 20 more years. Die and be happy. Next rebirth, even better. Keep up that sort of thing for one thousand more lifetimes until you reach nirvana and you need not have any guilt on your conscience. It is good to use your money to help others out, such as supporting charities but in this example, you are blameless. You've got a ticket to ride baby! Elite compassion.

Livelihood also means working to live in the world. It is noteworthy that the Buddha included work as one of the eight. Even though monks are supposed to live detached lives, the Buddha said that monks should have some work to do. Work is considered to be a part of your spiritual path, your spiritual practice. Work is not some cruel imposition upon us which we must undergo so that we can be spiritual beings on the weekends or on our time off. We practice mindfulness on the job and progress on the path while we work. Because work involves you in so many aspects of life, dealing with unpleasant people, learning new things, physical effort, right livelihood means that you are engaged with the world. You shouldn't just retreat into a cave or hide in a cheap basement suite, collecting welfare. Go out and get a job! There's no room in Buddhism to avoid getting a job because you're 'too spiritual.' The tendency to avoid work indicates a psychological tendency of avoidance behaviour altogether. You should work to pay your rent, buy food, get a bus pass, new socks, etc. Reality forces you to relate with the world, which is good. This trains you in mindfulness.

Some jobs are better for mindfulness than others. Enlightenment is more likely to come from sweeping a warehouse than closing deals on the phone. Manual labour gives you plenty of opportunities to practice meditation in action. You put your mind on what you are doing, as you are doing it. You mentally note to yourself "sweep, sweep, sweep." Tilopa, one of the great fathers of Tibetan Buddhism, worked crushing sesame seeds.

Right Effort

Right speech, discipline and livelihood constitute sila, the virtue stage of the path. The mental purific tion stage consists of the last three parts — right effort, mindfulness, and absorption. Effort is divided into four aspects of one thing:

1. exerting will to prevent unskilful states of mind from arising.
2. exerting will to dispel unwholesome, unskilful states of mind that have already arisen.
3. the will to cause wholesome, skillful states of mind to arise.
4. to develop and bring to perfection good, wholesome states of mind that are already present.

Right effort is what meditation is. Some people forget this. It is the will to fight unwholesome desire, the cause of suffering. Habitual patterns drive our passions and emotions but it is our noble efforts that drag our lives out of the slime and the muck of the dark age and into the light of wakefulness. Attaining nirvana takes tremendous effort and exertion. Prince Siddhartha practiced hard for six years. You can't just let go and attain enlightenment by going with the flow. It doesn't work that way. Meditation practice is hard work, like cleaning your house from top to bottom. Once Milarepa was passing on a teaching to his dharma heir, S. Gampopa. They were alone in the Tibetan wilderness and Gampopa was bidding him good-bye. Milarepa told him that he had a secret to share with him before he went. Gampopa waited attentively while Milarepa turned around and lifted his lower robe to reveal callouses all over his bottom. Gampopa really appreciated his message, and Milarepa told him that he wouldn't give that secret to just anyone.

Today Milarepa is the greatest folk hero in Tibetan history because of his effort. Because he had used black magic to kill people in his youth, he applied effort on the path, like no one else. Fear of his own bad karma propelled his efforts to benefit others. None of us have enough effort do we? We have so many gadgets that we just have to press a button to do some work. We click onto Google, then click on You Tube, then click onto our email. This can make us lazy at working with our minds. But human life is a workable situation. Materialism can be transformed into a spiritual advantage. You can curb your indulgence in materialism while benefitting greatly from comfort, health care, and efficiency. You can work on your spiritual path even in a mansion. You can do it! You don't have to blame the world for making you wealthy. You karmicly deserved the birth you had, and you can develop sincere heartfelt compassion for other rich people. You can overcome the encumbrances of prestige and wealth. The Buddha did and he taught that human birth is ideal for practicing the dharma.

Right Mindfulness

Right mindfulness continues the process of building concentration which leads to wisdom, insight. The Buddha once had a monk who told him that he couldn't memorize the many precepts, let alone practice them. The Buddha asked the monk "Can you do just one thing?" "Sure, what is it?" the monk asked. "Mindfulness," the Buddha replied. "Just practice mindfulness." Mindfulness is the most basic thing in Buddhism. Meditation is prime time mindfulness. Beyond the meditation cushion mindfulness should be applied in our ordinary existence as a way of life, a lifestyle of mindfulness. Through mindfulness on the ordinary, life becomes extraordinary. That is insight, pannya. Mindfulness comes from the Pali word 'sati' which means 'bare awareness' but mindfulness is more than paying attention and putting your mind on what you are doing. It also has the meaning of memory, actually; not the memory of the distant past but more the quality of recollection, recollecting the instructions, keeping something in mind, like wise instructions learned long ago. The reason why we can't keep those resolutions that we make for ourselves is that we keep forgetting to do it!

Right Absorption

Completing the stage of mental purification, the last on the eightfold path is right absorption. This means making efforts towards reaching a jhana. This is a state of one pointed concentration. A jhana state occurs when all five senses shut down in deep meditation. You have a black out. You can't feel your body below the neck, and then you can't feel your body at all. Your sense of hearing, smell, and taste shut down too. You still have thoughts in the first jhana and you are aware that you are having a wonderful experience, filled with rapture. Whereas a samadhi is a state of sustained attention on one object, with no breaks. Jhanas are deeper. There are four levels of jhana, then four immaterial jhanas, which aren't really necessary. The first four jhanas are necessary to obtain enlightenment. All eight jhanas were taught to Prince Siddhartha by master Uddaka Ramaputta, and he succeeded at all of them. But he found that such a state of mind was not enlightenment because after he came out of his absorption state he was still in the world of suffering, dukkha. A jhana doesn't last more than a few hours, usually but the Buddha called it a temporary nirvana. Ajahn Brahm, who is our famous jhana monk, says the five hindrances are suppressed in jhana like five relatives who are sleeping on your floor. Before they wake up your mind is completely clear and powerful and blissful. That is the time to practice true vipassana meditation to see into the true nature of things before your five guests rouse themselves and start to act up again.

After his enlightenment, Buddha taught the jhanas again and again. He endlessly praised them for happiness here and now and as a great support for insight. If you read the Pali suttas you will discover countless discourses where the Buddha brings the subject of his talk to what he called the first meditation. A paragraph is devoted to that, then the Buddha describes the second meditation, and so forth. A whole page will be devoted to all of these eight absorption states, and this pattern is repeated again and again in the suttas. Obviously the Buddha felt that it was important to do extensive practice of meditation, which is

normally required to reach a jhana. Even though it is not enlightenment, a jhana is the mark of a concentrated mind, a steppingstone to
enlightenment. Number eight is the most difficult part of the eightfold
path but you can't just skip it. You can't get into university without
completing grade 12. You can't leave it off. It's ridiculous to think
that someone could get enlightened without the jhanas because you
need that mental stabilization and powerful concentration to see into
these truths. Very few meditators will reach jhana in their entire lives.
Knowing this, some schools of thought minimize the importance of
jhana or even criticize it as unnecessary but this is what the Buddha
taught.

Ajahn Brahm gives some of the best teachings on jhanas based upon
his own experiences in his talks on a CD called *The Buddhist Path
of Serenity and Insight* from a ten day December, 1997 retreat, part
of which is in booklet form in *The Basic Method of Meditation,* from
Ajahn Brahm's monastery near Perth, Australia. Go to the Buddhist
Society of Western Australia at bswa.org . Here he describes the
process of nimittas arising which are signs in meditation, such as an
inner light that arises. It's not really a light but it's a real object on the
landscape of your mind. You patiently stay with the light nimitta and
it's blissful feeling and you follow it all the way down into the first
jhana. It's breathtaking to hear these deep, subtle and detailed teachings about how to get into the jhanas.

The Japanese word Zen is a translation from the Chinese Ch'an
which comes from dhyana which goes back to the term jhana. The
Buddha and his senior disciples would often take a break by picking a jhana and going into that state. They would rest and recharge
their batteries, then come out of jhana refreshed. The Buddha chose
to die in the fourth absorption, the arahant Anuruddha revealed, as
Anuruddha was there at the time.

At Vipassana meditation centres in Thailand and Burma, natives and
foreigners take month long meditation retreats or more, with the

intent of reaching a jhana. During my time at the Buddhist temple Wat Ram Poeng in northern Thailand, I was close to Westerners who may have succeeded in reaching the first jhana. I was impressed to hear people confirming from their direct experience what the Buddha taught about deep concentration. Buddha described the experience of the first absorption as "momentary and discursive thought, accompanied by joy and rapture." At Wat Ram Poeng we were trained to use a digital alarm clock when we were meditating with the deliberate aspiration to reach a jhana. The purpose was to check the clock from time to time because if you slip into a jhana you lose perception of time. For the first time in your life, thought actually comes to a standstill. In the scriptures this state is compared to the Ganges River. The Ganges is flowing along, a mile wide, then suddenly it stops! According to Carlos Castaneda, in his fictitious writings about the native Mexican Indian tradition, Don Juan called this 'stopping the world.'

We had a fellow named Volker on retreat at the monastery who was a former East German soldier. Near the end of his retreat he had been diligently practicing sitting and walking meditation for hours and hours. He sat outside his kuti (meditation house) at a table to take a break for a little bit, and the next thing he knew, the time on his watch had jumped forward an hour. He may have had a jhana. When a person takes a break and relaxes, this can help the process because they drop their struggle and just let be. After the Buddha's parinirvana, his faithful attendant Ananda was striving to attain enlightenment by doing intensive meditation practice. When Ananda took a break to lie down, just as his hand touched the mat, he attained to ultimate enlightenment!

Conclusion

That completes an overview of the Buddha's noble eightfold path. Diligently practice and develop all the parts of the path. The Buddha taught the most important things for people to know, to make practical progress in his dhamma. The Buddha was a practical teacher and he did not give information just to satisfy people's curiosity. Buddha once visited a group of monks that wasted too much time in speculative views. He was staying in a Simsapa forest in Kosambi near modern day Allahabad in northeastern India. Buddha gave a powerful message when he came out of the forest with a handful of leaves in his hand. He asked the monks "What do you think, O bhikkhus? Which is more? These few leaves in my hand or the leaves in the forest over here?" — "Sir, very few are the leaves in the hand of the Blessed One, but indeed the leaves in the Simsapa forest over here are very much more abundant."

"Even so, bhikkhus, of what I have known I have told you only a little, what I have not told you is very much more. And why have I not told you those things? Because they are not useful, they are not conducive to understanding suffering, the cause of suffering and the way to the end of suffering. That is why I have not told you those things." It is futile to try to guess everything the Buddha knew but refused to teach us but what was in those leaves in his hand? They included karma and rebirth and the realms of existence. He didn't leave that information on the forest floor. He taught that those teachings were necessary for the spiritual practice.

The blanket statement about the value of information, which the Buddha expressed with a few leaves in his hand, gives us a blunt message. We must not waste our time in meaningless pursuits. We are all going to die someday; who knows when? Now is the time to utilize the blessing of our human birth to makes strides along the eightfold path. Today's information age makes this sutta even more relevant to our lives. Thousands of hours are being spent studying details that are not relevant to waking us up. People study television reruns from the 1950s on You Tube, or the atmosphere of Saturn's moon Titan. People with masters degrees study more and more information so that they can get a Ph. D degree. This may be beneficial but the Buddha's point is that the priority must be on the vital few things that really matter, not the trivial many.

People need to study and apply dhamma to their human existence and upgrading their interpersonal skills, their warmth, and their wandering mind, rather than upgrading their degree. Another message in this teaching by the Buddha is that if you study thousands of those leaves on the trees you'll just become more crazy and confused and lost in speculation because the more you do that, the less you are paying attention to the few leaves in the Buddha's hand that can put you on the right track and really help you. Never forget the forth noble truth: there is a path, it is eightfold, to the cessation of suffering, to nirvana.

Wat Pho–Reclining Buddha, Bangkok, Thailand
Depicting the time of the Buddha's death (parinirvana)
and the beginning of Buddhist history

Chapter 4

Karma and Rebirth

*"Through right practice, you allow your
old kamma to wear itself out."*
Ajahn Chah

The Importance of Kamma and Rebirth
by Ajahn Sona

I'd like to speak about kamma* and rebirth. More particularly, rather than exploring the details of how kamma and rebirth "works," I will talk about historical Western attitudes to this idea, and address some important reasons for believing in it. I'm interested to integrate the traditional idea of kamma and rebirth into our modern views. To do so, I'll keep one eye on popular culture in the twenty-first century and (as a Theravada Buddhist) the other on the fifth century BC. I'm being somewhat brave because very few Western monks want to talk about this. How many Western monks have you ever heard give a talk about kamma and rebirth, except as a poetic attempt to explain it, or in psychological terms that would correspond to certain mental states? But I'm a very dyed-in-the-wool, traditional Theravada Buddhist and the nature of kamma and rebirth is the centre of the Buddha's teaching. No kamma, no rebirth — no Buddha's teaching! Therefore, I like to be bold about this, and say I *do* believe in rebirth and I *do* believe in karma in a very literal way.

* "Kamma" is Pali for the well-known Sanskrit word "karma."

It's good and refreshing to discuss this matter. Many teachers pussyfoot around this and for good reason. Why? Because it's not part of the history of Western thought. But if you look around, some of the most brilliant thinkers in the West don't have trouble with the notion of kamma and rebirth. Some don't find it to be illogical. In fact they actually favour it, although, as we are often wont to do it in the West, they usually modify it in their own way. Perhaps people like us, from the Western school system, often have more of a problem with rebirth than with kamma, but these two go hand in hand. I don't believe that you can make a sensible argument for kamma without rebirth.

First, I'll talk about why there is a tendency not to believe in this. Why would you have an assumption or a preference either way, especially in a post-Christian society? I could understand if you were a nineteenth century Catholic, but now many people don't think of themselves as Christian or particularly religious. Yet we have a way of thinking about things, and this way of thinking often goes unquestioned. There's huge residue in our structures of thought and logic and conviction about all kinds of things that are the result of 2000 years of Christianity in the West. We are in a sense like fish who are very surprised to discover that we swim in water. Because it's always been there, we often are not aware of the water of our intellectual environment. We're swimming in an intellectual environment — in the midst of myriad assumptions and suggestions — that has been handed to us.

One of the reasons why people are surprised at the idea of kamma and rebirth is that no authority figures in their life ever discussed it — their grade nine chemistry teacher didn't raise the issue, nor did their grade eight social studies teacher, or anybody else in their school system. Even if you think you are an independent thinker you'd be surprised how influential those twelve years of authority figures are. And then you go to university and there's no serious thought given to the matter there, either. Of course, you will get a history of Western intellectual ideas at university but very rarely will you find kamma and rebirth brought up. If your parents don't discuss the matter then it's likely that no authority figure in your whole life has discussed it, so it's not surprising that you'd be a little bit suspicious of this idea. I relate to my own experience, here, because when I started university I started in philosophy and I think the notion of rebirth came up — but I immediately dismissed it. Many reasons

A Short Walk On An Ancient Path

came to mind. I'm very interested to look back on it, now, because I have a very powerful conviction that this — kamma and rebirth — is in fact how things work. What I'm interested in is why I thought I had such clever reasons for dismissing it. As I look back, I realize that in a sense each person is really *in* a culture. You could say that we are somewhat culturally *hypnotised.* This is true for all cultures. That is, all of us to some degree — unless you're a very type of special person — are culturally subject to suggestion from our culture. Hypnotism works through a suggestion, and we're all somewhat suggestible, so it is not surprising that when a large mass of people and everything you see in the media etc., suggest certain ways of thinking, we tend to be deeply influenced by it. It is not just a matter of even-handedly receiving and sifting through everything that comes from your parents and the media and everyone around you.

Remember that slavery was abolished in the United States just a century and a half ago. The idea that very few thinkers in the United States before the 1860s really had a problem with human slavery is most astonishing, amazing! What is also very interesting is that you find thinkers who *did* have a problem with it. They were born and raised in their societies and given the same kind of misdirection, and cues. Yet when they reached an intellectual age in their late teens or twenties somehow they began to see, "These people who you are holding as slaves are fully human, you know. They really aren't a different species at all! There's something terribly wrong here." It's a very peculiar thing to awaken from hypnosis, surrounded by a sea of people in a hypnotic state. One of the people I like to read is Henry Thoreau who was an adult roughly from the 1830s to 1860s — before the abolition of slavery. When reading him on slavery you find he reacts just like we would. It's like he's living in the wrong time; he's a very modern person: *What in heaven's name is going on? Are you crazy?...* How did he escape the conditioning? By the way, I should mention that although he lived at that time in the middle of the United States when there weren't any alternatives to Christian ideas, Thoreau also had no problem with rebirth and karma. So, independent thinkers occasionally do arise. They are somehow able to examine current attitudes in a dispassionate way, to see through such concepts, and to go beyond the hypnotic influence of their prevailing culture.

Then again, it is surprising how suggestible some of the very famous thinkers in history have been when it comes to certain opinions. They're very clever and free-thinking, and what we agree in later ages to be far ahead of their time, but they do have their weaknesses. For instance, Socrates, Plato, and Aristotle didn't have a problem with slavery. Many well known people throughout history didn't have a particular problem with slavery. Even Christ didn't object specifically to it, saying, *Slaves obey your masters.* But it's interesting that the Buddha did have a problem with slavery. Over 2500 years ago he identified the ownership or traffic in human beings as one of the types of "wrong livelihood." He was also critical of the notion of caste in Indian society, and introduced a non-caste structure into the Sangha (monastic community). In addition, the Buddha accepted women as full participants in the holy life. Such instances reflect an amazing capacity to look beyond the prejudices of social conventions and ideas.

I'm bringing up these examples to encourage reflection on your own life and beliefs and political ideas, and to urge you to inquire: *Why do I think what I think? What's really going on here? Is it my mother or father, or the TV set, talking through my head? Am I really thinking for myself? Have I really examined these ideas?* These are important questions.

It is often held that the Buddha simply inherited the idea of rebirth or kamma from his culture, and that he chose not to dispute it in order to communicate other, more important, elements of his teaching. Many early investigators of Buddhism tended to assume that rebirth did not take place in any literal sense. In their reading of his teachings, the Buddha — whom many admired as a great psychologist and ethicist — referred to kamma and rebirth for one of two reasons. Either the Buddha was speaking figuratively, because he knew that rebirth and kamma did not occur but thought it was a valuable teaching to get people out of suffering, or he had uncritically absorbed this attitude from his time and culture. Perhaps we come across these assumptions less commonly nowadays but one frequently encounters them in early Western presentations of the Buddha. Yet when you read through the entire Pali Canon and its commentaries, and examine the history of that time, you see that these modern interpretations hold no water.

The fifth century BC is one of the richest centuries in all of history, certainly the most influential century to date — far more so than say the sixteenth through nineteenth centuries. There's no question if you compare it. Who was alive during the fifth century BC? Sometimes I like to ask people: *how many people can you name from the fifth century BC, quickly?* You can probably name a few from the nineteenth century like Abraham Lincoln but how many can you name from the fifth century BC? You might be surprised: Confucius, Lao Tzu, Socrates, Plato, the Buddha. The twentieth century philosopher Alfred North Whitehead once observed, "All of Western philosophy is a footnote to Plato." Whether it's true or not, we're obviously still talking about Plato and we've forgotten many thinkers who came in between. It's remarkable how we're still playing out those ideas from the fifth century BC. I sometimes give talks in high schools and once I was speaking to six classes of Grades 8s in Penticton, BC. There were 180 of them, and I asked them "How many of you have heard of the Buddha?" Remember, this is in a non-Buddhist country 2500 years after the Buddha, and eighth-graders are not known for their learnedness in history. Yet all but *one* had heard of the Buddha (and I think she just wanted attention!). I asked how many had heard of Socrates. Five. This is amazing because it's not being pushed on every street corner or anything. I heard a story about one of Ajahn Viradhammo's students who was a photographer. One day he was in a church to take some photos, accompanied by his twelve year old daughter. She had never been in a church before and was wandering around looking at everything. After a while she came up to him and said, "Dad! There's a guy up there who's been shot!" Looking at the wall, he said "What?! You know what this is!" — "Well he's shot or something; he's bleeding out the side," she explained. "Don't you know what that is?" he said, "That's Jesus!" She had never heard of him. We take this for granted, but unless you're deliberately exposed to the story it's possible to be twelve years old, and never hear of Jesus!

To return to my point, more or less the whole range of possible views that we have received through Western thinkers was available and carefully examined during the Buddha's time. The fifth century BC was a rich century that contained some very bright people with all kinds of interesting ideas. As a result, the notion that everyone in India during the Buddha's time believed in rebirth just isn't true. The Buddha was in regular debate with various people around him who didn't think such things. For instance, he explicitly examines and argues with what are traditionally called "teachers of six different schools," which pretty well covers all the possibilities. One school, the materialist, or annihilationist, school is precisely what many people believe in modern times. That was a well known course of thought in that time. What is an annihilationist? That is a person who believes that a person lives, eventually dies, and that's it. It's finished. The Buddha was very familiar with this view and he explicitly rejected it. He said, "This is a false doctrine. I do not believe this." There were people who held the view that your life is predestined; they considered free will an illusion and that you were completely conditioned and predestined. He rejected that view. There were those who claimed that what happened to you in life was without cause — completely chaotic and random. He rejected that view. Also the notion that external forces completely control the way you think. He rejected that view. Another view held that you could influence your life by rituals, in other words, that you could change your fate by ritually influencing a god through some means or another. The Buddha rejected that as well.

We're starting to go through most of the possibilities in life. Of course, the big fork in the road is: you die or you don't, right? So that's the first big fork in the road. If you decide that you just die, then there's no more discussion. There aren't too many variations with this, nothing to talk about. There's not two ways of annihilation; there's only one way. But if it's possible that you persist after death, there are several interesting variations. For example, some people believed that you persist but your present life has no influence on the quality of the life after death. What you thought or did or said in a life had no relevance or effect on the life that follows. Other possibilities are that it has a complete conditioning effect, or only a partial conditioning effect. All of these views were examined by the Buddha as well.

There is an early Buddhist discourse that offers a very detailed examination of virtually every possible mode of thought that you can find examined in philosophy, up to the present. It's called the "Discourse on the Great Net of Views, the Brahmajala Sutta" in the *Longer Length Sayings* (*Digha Nikaya*). The Buddha says that the sixty-two views he describes and examines comprise all the possible views. In this discourse he recounts them systematically, examining the faults and inconsistencies in each case. So, again, the notion that the Buddha just drifted along with the general thought of the time — that is, that he was an uncritical product of his culture — is *way off.*

Nevertheless, this has been proposed, especially by some Western lay teachers who have an admiration for the teachings of the Buddha but do not have very much knowledge about the suttas themselves. They may have never read what he said. Because knowledge of the teachings of the Buddha is not widespread in the West teachers could once easily get away with this. As time passes, though, more people in the West are becoming informed and there are more lucid and accurate translations of what the Buddha said. People are reading it for themselves. It's no longer enough to have been on one's first six week retreat in Asia, then to return as a fully qualified teacher. It doesn't go that way anymore because people know a little bit more. I find that some of the Western monks are now very well educated and thoroughly knowledgeable about the suttas and they are trying to correct some of the misapprehensions that have been passed off in the West. The ones that I'm more impressed with are talking about the nature of kamma and rebirth as a literal idea of the Buddha.

Then again, I fully understand why there should be resistance to teaching kamma and rebirth as literally true. When you're trying to present this to people you recognize that in our culture there's going to be a strong resistance to the notion — people have just never heard about it, so they will naturally struggle with it. In addition, there is great benefit to meditation. Psychologically it's such a relief from suffering. It can be admitted that you don't have to believe in karma and rebirth to get a lot of benefit, psychological relief, from these marvellous techniques created by the Buddha. Therefore it's not difficult to see why, when presenting Buddhist teachings, a teacher might want to avoid a lot of initial resistance in order for people to begin to receive some benefit from the practice.

The Buddha himself often presented his teachings this way. If he felt that an audience would be highly resistant to some notions, he set them aside. He said, in effect: *It's like a smörgåsbord that I'm offering you. Eat whatever you like. If you just like olives, go for the olives. I'm just happy for you.* It's like being a kid where you don't want to eat certain things. Eventually, though, you widen your palate. You realize: I've really missed out on some good stuff. In a sense, the Buddha is just a kindly person who knows human nature and is very compassionately interested that people benefit in any way they can. He realizes that the mind shuts down on certain things but is open to other things, so the Buddha employs what are called skilful teachings. skilful teachings require a certain degree of assessment. A teacher needs to find out what might be useful for an audience. I find in my own experience in the West and inquiry into the history of teaching in the West for the last 40 years, that there's a degree of "spoon feeding" that often occurs, hoping not to upset anybody by mentioning certain things. That works for a while, but at some point you have to respect people, particularly the boomer generation who now are about 45 to 65. Which is to say that if you don't offer it to them now, I don't know when you will be able to do so. As a result, it is important that one present the full range of the Buddha's teachings in a very straightforward way saying, *you may have heard some of this in your meditation course and you may have just enjoyed the breath and so forth but, really, there is another, larger dimension to these teachings which are intrinsically important.*

Why should we introduce kamma and rebirth if one can get benefits from meditation without taking these ideas on board? Because the benefits of meditative techniques — for instance, the cultivation of loving kindness, compassion, and altruistic joy — are profoundly useful and helpful at a social level and healing to the individual's psyche but in themselves they don't offer enough. You might say that there isn't enough "fuel" within these practices to push you to enlightenment.

Remember that the Buddha was interested to come to the end of suffering. What did he consider to be suffering — just aches and pains in this life? What was the Buddha's problem with suffering? Why was he so disturbed about aging, sickness and death? Particularly if it's *over* when you die… that's not that so bad! What could be the problem? The reason is that he did not think you simply die. The problem is you just get born again because you haven't understood the nature of your drives, what drives you through existence. He asks us, what is the cause of suffering? Old age, sickness and death, grief, sorrow, lamentation? Is that what the cause is? No, that's what suffering is; that's the first noble truth. The cause of suffering is attachment, so even if you could superficially treat aging, sickness, and death, that's not going to ease suffering. Then again, from an annihilationist point of view, if the cause of suffering is attachment this should end when you die, right? But the Buddha pointed out that we don't get over attachment by dying. We have to uproot it with wisdom.

The four noble truths — that there is suffering, that there is a cause of suffering, that there is an end to suffering, and that there is a way (the eightfold path) to the end of suffering — don't have any coherence if you do not include the notion that the real problem carries on beyond this life. If death was the end of suffering you wouldn't need an eightfold path. You would just die and (or, *so the thinking might go*) maybe the sooner the better. Indeed, this is one of the repercussions of a strongly held annihilationist view. One might think: *well, it's starting to get painful here — I think I'll just end my suffering.* That's an argument that has been percolating through society: euthanasia might be a good idea, a very accessible and easy way for one to die and get over suffering. A compassionate person might advocate this. Why does the Buddha so object to this conclusion? It's relevant to note that Buddhist monks are forbidden to advocate suicide to anybody, even for compassionate reasons. If a monk does suggest the idea, and someone acts on it, that monk is immediately disrobed and can never be a monk for the rest of his life. That's how seriously the Buddha views this suggestion. Buddhist monks are supposed to be compassionate so why would the Buddha forbid them from making this suggestion? Why does he object to euthanasia? *Because such compassion is based on the idea that death ends suffering.*

It's built very deeply into Buddhist teaching that death is not the solution to suffering. Therefore kamma and rebirth have vital repercussions beyond what you might think. These realities affect all kinds of political discussions and sociological views about how life works and what the best way to deal with society is, and so forth. Belief in kamma and rebirth will shape your entire view of life. I don't see any other viewpoint that gives meaning to life like kamma and rebirth.

Some people say that religious people who believe that you persist after death have wishful thinking — they're actually afraid of death and they just make up a story because they just can't face the truth. But actually, many religious people would argue just the opposite; they would say that death-as-the-end would actually be easy. You would just die and that's it — no responsibility for your actions and no further suffering, no worries. That is not a difficult possibility to face. The idea that when you die, it's over, is *not at all* a courageous conviction — that's the easy conviction. That's why it's appealing. People would prefer to not worry about it. It would be so nice if nothing that I did in my life mattered one way or the other. I would be off the hook; I wouldn't have to concern myself about this. In fact, there's a strong temptation to take up the view that death is the end because there's no responsibility.

Conversely, the view of continuation after death leaves you with responsibility — or at least the possibility, because there are two kinds of views here: One possibility is that what you did in life will have repercussions after this life. The other is that there is continuation but there is no moral connection between this life and the next. You can see that the second view undermines responsibility. If there is no connection in the next life with your actions in this life, it tends to make this life a little absurd. Whatever you do doesn't matter.

The Buddha criticized a contemporary teacher who held this view in a very strong way. This teacher denied the moral results of actions. He taught that if you slaughtered beings on one side of the Ganges River and caused others to slaughter, and then gave out gifts on the other side of the Ganges River and caused others to give gifts, there would be no moral result to either of your actions. None. We might ask what would motivate a person to teach that? If nothing matters why does he care? The Buddha was well aware of this view and utterly rejected it. The Buddha is a very rational, logical thinker, and he finds it unskilful to believe that the events in your life are meaningless, that they're causal but lack any intrinsic moral dimension. It's as if something falls on your head then gravity caused it, but there's no other reason beyond that. That's a very common view these days as well: that things happen for a reason but not one with any kind of moral dimension. The Buddha is saying, *no: physical laws are not removed from moral laws.* There is a complex inter-relation among the laws of kamma, cause and effect, psychological laws, biological laws, and physical laws. It's very complex but there is intrinsic meaning to it all. He's holding that psychological wholeness is missing if you do not see that intentional ethical actions have consequences, and that what happens to you in this life is a result of previous ethical actions. If you remove the vital dimension of meaning, this creates a dizziness in life, a psychological sense that life is slightly absurd and meaningless. Your inner being feels a deflation or vertigo. There's a famous novel by Satre called *Nausea*. What is the cause of that nausea? One of the pervasive feelings dominant in the West, with science, is that what you do is not meaningful, it doesn't have any consequences. When this hits the

A Short Walk On An Ancient Path

psyche it has a dizzying effect, a feeling that you're in a completely direc-tionless vacuum — that nothing means anything. One of the things to ask, here, is, if this — the lack of moral consequence — is true, why would you care? After all, in a non-moral vacuum, the door is open for one to reject the truth as well. If the truth is that nothing matters, why would one think the *truth* matters? In response, you may jump to the conclusion that it's important to know the truth. But it can only be important if the truth implies that it's important to know the truth. If not, who cares?

The truth is not something abstract; it's not separate from a sense of meaning. That is what the Buddha said again and again: "I don't always tell the truth, but I don't tell a lie. I only say what is true and beneficial." If the truth is not beneficial then why say it? Do you want benefit or truth? I'll take the benefit any day. And again, if there are no consequences to any action, what is the problem with a false view? Why would you insist on truth?

This is what the Buddha actually says to a group of intelligent questioners known as the Kalamas. They asked him to provide good criteria to distin-guish between the conflicting truth claims made by various teachers of the day. The Buddha pointed out that no reward could possibly be derived from the belief that death is final. None at all. This is because if you're annihilated you can never find out you were right. But what happens if you're wrong? *Bad mistake.* For one thing, you've experienced nausea and confusion in life owing to your conviction that nothing is meaningful. So the Buddha urges his listeners to bet heavily on moral meaning and continua-tion — kamma and rebirth. Note that he is not suggesting that one claims knowledge one doesn't have. Rather, he's saying that to have the *convic-tion* is utterly health producing.

The conviction that everything you do and think and say is consequen-tial and meaningful is not lost in the universe. What happens to you in life is not random, bizarre, or irrational. It is meaningful and governed by causes in the ethical dimension, not just the physical. Bet heavily on this. The consequences of being wrong are nil, literally nil. If you are annihilated you cannot *talk* about the meaningfulness of life. All of the actions you have done would just dribble off into nothingness. There are all kinds of people in prison who have done terrible things, and there are people out of prison who have done terrible things who, in this life, are not experiencing any consequences related to those events. On the

Karma and Rebirth

face of things, it's very hard to make any sense of it. It's simply not the case that things always work out justly in this life. So take that sense of meaningfulness seriously; most people don't think about this very much. Instead, most people seek happiness, even though they often don't do it skilfully. So the Buddha is proposing an overarching, ultimate view of reality called kamma and rebirth.

'Kamma' means that every intentional action has a consequence and that this life is but one in a series of lives without conceivable beginning. Only with this view can you come to a comprehensive sense of structure in life. Anything short tends to be diminished in terms of a deep structure of meaning, perfect symmetry, and lawfulness. That's why you want to go beyond meditation techniques like the cultivation of loving kindness, or serenity and concentration developed through breath meditation. These techniques are very powerful and contribute directly to your emotional and psychological improvement, yet they will only go to a point and then stop because the energy that can drive them any further is absent. The energy needed to propel one's practice beyond this is a conviction — not the knowledge but the *conviction* — of kamma and rebirth. It's the only thing that drives practice beyond, which is why it is vital on occasion to really think about this subject.

There are many good talks on meditation and so forth but I very rarely have heard a straight talk on kamma and rebirth, even in monasteries. It's good from time to time to really think about it, not tippy toe around it, and to realize that it really is a very important dimension of the teachings of the Buddha — something he teaches again and again. It doesn't mean that you have to try to force it on everyone who walks into a mindfulness course. This is not skilful. You have to assess your audience. But it is also not skilful or honest to pretend that it is not a part of the teaching of the Buddha, because some people in that audience may have the capacity to really intuit these ideas, and this conviction can push them to a new level of understanding, wisdom, and well-being. I happen to be one of those people. I'm really glad that somebody mentioned rebirth and kamma. As I've said, my initial assessment of the whole matter was skeptical. My character is logical and rational and I'm educated in the Western systems, so I had lots of interesting arguments this way and that way against it. Eventually I came around to a full conviction of it. There's nothing irrational about it. There are lots of very intelligent, well

A Short Walk On An Ancient Path

qualified people who believe it. There have been a couple of monks in my monastery who have Ph. Ds from Western universities, one in hard science. They're deeply convinced of the notion of kamma and rebirth. We don't have a problem with it at all. We don't pretend it's a story or anything like that.

It's not like believing in God. The arguments for and against the existence of God are entirely different from the teachings on kamma and rebirth. The Buddha does not argue for or against the existence of God, in fact, he's not particularly interested. He doesn't find it to be a question that will cause well-being, nor motivate one towards a reduction of suffering through the cessation of attachment. That's why Buddhism can be seen to offer a very different view from purely theistic religions in this respect.

To conclude this talk on kamma and rebirth, I trust I have made it clear that these principles are taught by the Buddha and are intrinsic to our making sense of his teachings. If you hope to attain what the Buddha called enlightenment, liberation, or freedom, you cannot possibly do so without a conviction in rebirth and kamma. It is one of the characteristics that accompanies even the first stage of enlightenment: a complete conviction in the teachings of the Buddha, including "This is right view, the belief in kamma and rebirth." This is stated by the Buddha unequivocally.

The Buddha left it wide open; you don't have to believe any of this. Yet he's saying, in essence: "I'll tell you what — it's very profitable to have a conviction about kamma and rebirth. You will feel the sense of health and well-being and sanity that comes from this conviction." The Buddha is not suggesting that one should claim knowledge, or that we should simply wish or hope that it's true. However, real benefit comes from taking it on as a conviction, betting on a view that has no down side to it. You see, we're in a genuine predicament: we're thrust into life. This is the game that must be played. Sometimes you don't want to play the game but you have to anyway. It's one of those games you just can't get out of. You know those games at school, when you say, "I don't want to play today," and everybody lets you not play? Life is not one of those; it makes you play. You cannot get out of making choices. That's the only thing about which you have no choice whatsoever. And these choices have to be made in the absence of knowledge. No one steps out of the door in the morning knowing what's going to happen to them;

this uncertainty is part of being human. You get out there and you make choices, quick choices, continuous decisions, without full knowledge of the facts. You're thrust into that situation again and again, and you have to make these decisions as best as possible from what you know and can determine, from what you guess or intuit. That's how you make decisions; it's also how you make convictions. And I say that you risk your life in the process: Whatever you bet, you bet your life. Whatever you do, you bet your life. Every time you make a decision or a choice, you bet your life. It's interesting to discover what the Buddha, who after 2500 years is still remembered by 179 grade eights in Penticton, BC, had to say about this. It's valuable to consult such a source, when asking a question like, *what I should bet my life on?*

(From a 2003 talk in Ottawa, transcribed by Brian Ruhe, edited by Venerable Pavaro)

Evidence for Karma and Rebirth

Before briefly giving evidence for karma and rebirth I'll outline some details of how karma and rebirth works, then there is a more thorough treatment of rebirth by Bhikkhu Bodhi. The word karma is more familiar to people than kamma so I tend to use that. Karma is a word that has become part of the English language. On the bus where I live in Vancouver, BC they have recycling ads with a cartoon showing a couple on a twin bicycle. As they are riding, the lady on the back seat tosses an empty bottle away. In the next frame an old CCCP satellite falls from the sky and crashes upon just her. The caption reads "Don't mess with karma!"

Look at the multitude of beings living on the planet. There's a wide array of animals and people. Why do beings take rebirth in a particular form? Is it by luck, by accident or chance or is there a principle underlying the process? In philosophy, there are three ways to explain how the universe generally works. One, is that this is a random, causeless universe. Things happen for no reason at all; bad things happen to good people. It's just a fool's delight! How does that make

A Short Walk On An Ancient Path

you feel? The second is, there's a God that decides on everything and he crushes AIDS babies into the dirt for his sport. The third is that things happen for a reason, the law of cause and effect and karma. This gives you control over your life because even in the worst times, you can still choose to do the right thing and make good karma.

Perhaps the most important question in life is "What happens after we die?" You might dismiss this, thinking that you will wait and find out, but if you deeply consider how your beliefs effect your actions you will see that your views about an afterlife determine how you act right now in this life. For example the three positions on human destiny after death are:

1. There is no afterlife. Human consciousness is just a product of the brain so when the brain and body die, you are annihilated.
2. The theistic view in orthodox Christianity, Judaism and Islam believes that after just this one lifetime on earth you go to an eternal heaven or hell depending upon your present actions and beliefs.
3. Rebirth. Variations in this view are in Buddhism and Hinduism and now over half of the world's population believe in rebirth, including the non-religious, the new age, and even some sects of Muslims. This is the idea that this life is just one link in a chain of lives going back into the beginningless past and forward into the future.

If a person takes the materialist view, they will believe that there will be no moral consequences to their actions after they die. They will be extinguished and will feel no pain or pleasure because of what they have done on Earth. This view may encourage someone to focus on grasping as much sensual pleasure in this life because there is no spiritual path to build upon in a future life. They might be tempted into greed, cheating or worse if there are no consequences to their actions. Many of my friends and family members share this view and they are just as moral as people who believe there will be consequences after death. The second view puts more emphasis on a person's relationship with God and trying to appease God to obtain admittance to heaven. The third view of rebirth makes one feel more responsible for his or her actions as they believe they are going to come back to them.

Rebirth in Buddhism is the view that when you die you are immediately reborn in another form. Karma is defined as the mental intention that initiates any action. Understanding the principle of karma is simple enough. If you do good actions, that will result in happy states of mind and better conditions in the future. If you do negative actions, that will result in unhappy states of mind and unpleasant conditions in the future. The Buddha said "Monks it is volition that I call kamma. For having willed, one then acts by body, speech or mind". What is behind action is volition; the impetus is the will. Intentional actions manifesting through body, speech and mind are what the Buddha calls kamma. This means that actions without intention are not kamma. If you're walking down the sidewalk and you step on an ant without even being aware of it, then there's no karma. You didn't break the precept against killing because you had no intention to kill (you could say that it was the ant's karmic result to die at that time). Also, if you hear something from a friend and repeat it to someone but later find out that it's not true, that's not the karma of lying because you didn't have the intention to deceive.

Karma comes through the three "gates" of body, speech and mind. We affect the world with our acts and our speech too; but just at a level of thought, if we have a sustained thought, a sustained intention, like desiring inwardly, planning, aspiring, we have mental karma. What lies behind all of this is intention and the Buddha said that mind is the forerunner of all. The Buddha defeated the leader of the Jains in a debate on this point. The Jain teacher said that actions of the body are more important than actions of the mind. The Buddha said no, actions of the mind are more important because when you accidentally step on an insect, the body kills it but the mind had no such intention, so it is the intention of the mind that determines the weight of the karma, not the body.

There are ten main forms of unwholesome actions:

Bodily
1. Taking life
2. Taking what does not belong to oneself
3. Engaging in sexual misconduct (adultery, seduction, etc.)

Verbal
4. Speaking falsehood
5. Speaking slanderous speech
6. Speaking harshly
7. Engaging in idle chatter, in gossip

Mental
8. Covetousness,yearning for the possessions of others
9. Ill will (Actively desiring harm, suffering and destruction to come to others)
10. Wrong views (specially fixed wrong views which deny the efficacy of moral action.)

By abstaining from the above, you develop the opposite virtues, the ten courses of wholesome action.

Bhikkhu Bodhi states (Bodhi, 1984):

According to the Buddha, our willed actions produce effects. They eventually return to ourselves. One effect is the immediately visible psychological effect. The other is the effect of moral retribution.

Firstly let us deal with the psychological effect of kamma. When a willed action is performed it leaves a track in the mind, an imprint which can mark the beginning of a new mental tendency. It has a tendency to repeat itself, to reproduce itself, somewhat like a protozoan, like an amoeba. As these actions multiply, they form our character. Our personality is nothing but a sum of all our willed actions, a cross-section of all our accumulated kamma. So by yielding first in simple ways to the unwholesome impulses of the mind, we build up little by little a greedy character, a hostile character, an aggressive character or a deluded character. On the other hand, by resisting these unwholesome desires we replace them with their opposites, the wholesome qualities. Then we develop a generous character, a loving and a compassionate personality, or we can become wise and enlightened beings. As we change our habits gradually, we change our character, and as we change our character we change our total being, our whole world. That is why the Buddha emphasizes, so strongly the need to be mindful of every action, of every choice. For every choice of ours has a tremendous potential for the future.

Seen from this angle, from the standpoint of karmic law, the universe appears to maintain a certain moral equilibrium, a balance between all the morally significant deeds and the objective situations of those who perform them. So the law of kamma is a moral application of the general principle that for every action there is an equal and an opposite reaction.

What is so difficult about karma is seeing the exact details of how it works. Karma has three components: actions, their effects and their potentialities. Action has to do with the law of cause and effect. Karma is a special instance of the law of cause and effect which is the master law of the universe. Everything happens according to natural laws. Not a leaf falls from a tree except by law. The way the earth orbits around the sun is not karma; there's no being there. It's just cause and effect. So karma is the law of cause and effect in the moral dimension. For these three components, action means what you intentionally do now in the present moment. Karma always means in the present moment. The effects are the results of karma which can come much later. This means that karma is waiting for an opportunity to ripen. The lag time between these two is the potentialities which exist in your mental continuum. Someone asked the Buddha if kamma is stored in the body or the mind. The Buddha pointed at a mango tree without any fruit and the Buddha asked, "Where are the mangoes stored"? The man explained that they weren't stored anywhere, they just hadn't developed yet and then the Buddha pointed out that karma is the same way.

Karma has a tendency to develop like seeds pushing for an opportunity to sprout. It's as if we have white seeds and black seeds

A Short Walk On An Ancient Path

representing our good and bad karma. Like seeds scattered on the ground and on the rocks, not all seeds necessarily ripen. It's not a mathematical certainty that karma must ripen because karma is willed action, which is alive and organic. It is subject to the play of living forces and there's a lot of room for variation. The Buddha described three time periods in which karmas ripen. Some are due to ripen in this lifetime, some in the next lifetime and some in any lifetime after that and the third is the most powerful. This type stays with us until we reach nirvana so its results can come even after thousands of aeons in the future. Buddha taught "Tears you have shed, transmigrating and wandering, greater than the water in the four great oceans". If you have negative karmas that are due to ripen in this lifetime, but you practice virtue and stay on the side of the angels, then that negative karma may not find an opportunity to ripen. Thus when you die it gets cut off and becomes defunct karma. It's the same with the next lifetime too. Your good conduct could even influence your good karma to ripen and flower in this lifetime. The opposite is also true. If you break your precepts and fall into a bad crowd and get into the bad stuff, you may cut off some of your good karma that was due to come to you in this life while allowing negative karma to ripen. So, the ripening of our past karma is not just a passive process that happens to us, because how we act now can affect this dynamic. One karma can even be destroyed by another karma. A weighty karma is so strong that it will ripen no matter what we do.

The Buddha explained how the past life karmas of people caused huge variations in their fortunes.

- Killing in the past life results in being short lived in this life.
- Having a long life is the result of abstaining from killing and being kind and compassionate, having respect and reverence for life.
- Being sickly comes from injuring and hurting other beings.
- Being healthy comes to one who helped others, who gave and assisted others.

- Being angry results in one appearing ugly in this life.
- Being patient and cheerful in your past life make you beautiful in this life.
- People who are rich were generous in past lives.
- Being poor happens to people who were selfish.
- An influential person with authority rejoiced in the good fortune and success of others.
- A weak and powerless individual without any authority was envious of the good fortune of others, begrudging the honour, respect and veneration given them.
- Being intelligent comes from being reflective and studious, someone who always inquired and investigated matters. So it is good to ask questions of teachers.
- Being dull minded and stupid results from being lazy and negligent in the past, someone who never studied or applied much thought.
- Suffering from hunger results from stealing.
- Being in poverty comes from obstructing others from gaining their livelihood.
- Being with a great group of friends and then being separated from them is a result of seducing others partners or alienating their friends.

You can see the logic in the cause — effect relationship between our past life and this life. *Most* of our experiences are caused from actions committed in past lives.

I always get tough questions like, what about small children who starve to death in Africa, or what about people who are born crippled? Is that because of bad karma? Many teachers choose to answer the question indirectly, depending on the audience. I think the view of karma is that such people are suffering the results of past life karma. They may be very good hearted people and may have been in their past five lifetimes as well, but in a life before that they have made some mistakes and done the wrong thing and now they are feeling the result of that. It's not possible to be murdered unless you created the karmic cause in the past. It could even reduce your stress believing that you are paying off a karmic debt and knowing that you will be rewarded for your good actions. The mystery is when! Understanding the principle of karma is easy but the Buddha taught that you shouldn't try to figure out exactly how karma works in particular situations because it is so complex and subtle that it is one of the four imponderables. If you dwell on it too much it will lead you to vexation, drive you crazy and your head will explode into seven pieces, the Buddha taught, although I'm not aware of any case, in the suttas, of that actually happening. Now that you're wondering, the other three imponderables are: The range of a Buddha's mind — how much does the Buddha know? What is the extent of his psychic powers? And the range of the jhanic mind — how powerful is the mind of a meditator in the meditation absorption states? Then, there is pondering about the origin of things — did the universe have a beginning? Has it always been here? How far back does it go? It staggers the imagination. Don't go there, the Buddha says. You'll never figure it out. You would have to be a Buddha to see the direct cause and effect relationship built into karma.

People ask me, who decides? Who decides where you go when you die? I have a dry sense of humour so sometimes I say that there is a committee of monks in Bangkok who receive applications from people after they die, and then they decide. Then I stop myself and say that it is a natural law, like gravity. It happens automatically and the result of a wholesome or unwholesome action is built right into the action itself even though the result could take lifetimes to ripen. This doesn't mean that the result will be the same thing, but roughly equivalent. If you take care of your elderly mother for a year that doesn't mean that your daughter will take of you the same way but you will be rewarded for what you did, have confidence in that. As Ajahn Sona says, karma and rebirth really is the overarching ultimate view of reality. I agree that this is the view and the only view that gives meaning and purpose to life.

In *Wings to Awakening: An Anthology from the Pali Canon,* by Thanissaro Bhikkhu (Geoffrey DeGraff, 1999: 37) in the section, "Kamma & the Ending of Kamma" he writes:

> The Buddha's doctrine of kamma takes the fact of skillful action, which can be observed on the ordinary sensory level, and gives it an importance that, for a person pursuing the Buddhist goal, must be accepted on faith. According to this doctrine, skillful action is not simply one factor out of many contributing to happiness: it is the primary factor. It does not lead simply to happiness within the dimensions of time and the present: if developed to the ultimate level of refinement, it can lead to an Awakening totally released from those dimensions. These assertions cannot be proven prior to an experience of that Awakening, but they must be accepted as working hypotheses in the effort to develop the skillfulness needed for Awakening. This paradox — which lies at the heart of the act of taking refuge in the Triple Gem — explains why the serious pursuit of the Buddhist path is a sustained act of faith that can become truly firm only with the first glimpse of Awakening, called stream-entry. It also explains why a strong desire to gain release from the stress and suffering inherent in conditioned existence is needed for such a pursuit, for without that desire it is very difficult to break through this paradox with the necessary leap of faith.

Evidence for Rebirth

Karma and rebirth is not just a religious belief. From a Buddhist view there is evidence all over the place. Look at your tendencies, your talents and abilities and your phobias. Some of this may have been carried over from a previous life. Even though the vast majority of people don't remember their previous lives, past life memories are implicit, not explicit. You learned how to write but you don't remember how you learned. Nature is efficient that way. As a child you are not learning new things, you are remembering skills cultivated in a previous life so it's alright at age 75 to take up learning music. This is why you want the dhamma deeply embedded into your mind so it will stay with you. It's very scary to be lost without any spiritual direction. In your next life your mind will not feel at peace, it will keep searching until it finds the dhamma again. Then it will feel at home, "this is it".

The best scientific evidence for rebirth comes from the work of Dr. Ian Stevenson at the University of Virginia. He was a Canadian psychiatrist who read newspaper articles in the late 1950's about children in Asia who claimed to remember a previous life. This caught his interest and he then devoted the rest of his life to this research from 1960 until his death in 2007. He was concerned that his work would die with him because it wasn't popular there, in Virginia, in the Bible belt to practically prove that the Buddhist and Hindu views about rebirth are right, but the Christian, Jewish and Muslim teachings are wrong. He should have been on the *Oprah Winfrey* show. I and others and our monks are working to keep the results of his work alive. The work continues today with other doctors carrying on the research so the future looks good as this understanding gains wider acceptance.

A typical case is of a little boy or girl, after they begin to talk, around the age of two, three or four and they speak about experiences they had in a previous life. Sometimes they know just a few details, sometimes they talk incessantly about it and they want to get back to their previous family. It seems that about one out of 10,000 little kids have very clear recall about their previous life. This very compelling evidence I first heard about from Ajahn Sona. Many of our other monks such as Ajahn Brahm and Ajahn Jayasaro refer to Dr. Ian Stevenson as well because this is not Buddhism, this is medical science. This comes from the department of Psychiatry at a major American University. As Buddhists we can refer to this great body of over 3000 cases as scientific evidence for the Buddhist teachings on rebirth. You can find more info on this in the reference section of the reading list at the back of this book, or if you do an Internet search on Ian Stevenson you can find many cases and it takes you to the appropriate section of the University of Virginia website. I think he deserved the Noble prize in science.

What Dr. Ian Stevenson found is that in the vast majority of cases when a person dies, they immediately take rebirth in the ghost realm. Assuming that a person is not a serial killer or a total saint, the great majority will take rebirth as a ghost for some period of time. The Buddhist teachings do not specify for how long; it could be a few weeks or a few centuries. It depends upon a person's karma but Ian Stevenson found an average turn around time of one to three years from the time of death until the time someone comes out of the womb in their next human birth. The Buddha described the ghost realm as a highly varying realm, almost up to the heavenly world and almost down to the hell realm. One's future experience of being a ghost depends upon their individual karma. They may find the ghost realm reasonably pleasant, similar to their current state of mind. They could be hanging out with their ghost friends and entertaining themselves or their experience could be unpleasant and mixed. Many ghosts wander around in a somnambulistic sleep walking state, not aware of what is happening or even that they are dead. Some are attached to their house, possessions or family. There are photographs of ghosts of people who lived in a house for decades, died in the same house and when the new owner downloads film of a photo of the bedroom, they see the image of the ghost of the person who lived there before, even though they didn't see it when they took the picture.

It makes sense to have to spend some time in the ghost realm because when you die, there's not likely a womb available immediately, in the area. Another important result of Dr. Stevenson's research is that people tend to get reborn within about fifty miles from where they died. The distance varies in different parts of the world. There are many cases of Japanese soldiers in Burma who were killed in World War two and they took rebirth right there in Burma, close to where they died. Many of them identified with Japan, wanted to be in Japan and one little boy even spoke Japanese! One boy said to his impoverished parents "I'll go to Japan and get some money. I'll go to Tokyo and bring back some money." Why didn't they take rebirth in Japan if that's what they identified with? Because most people take rebirth close to where they died and these guys were struck there; it was their karma. There are great exceptions to this but if you go on vacation to Argentina and you slip on a banana peel and die there, then you will likely get reborn right there and have to learn Spanish. So now you have an idea about what's going to happen to you and your loved ones after you die. I want you to get your money's worth out of this book.

The reason why some people can be reborn within weeks is because there are several cases of someone dying, then bumping out a spirit already in a womb, and taking over that body — a form of permanent possession. In Thailand, in the case of Sergeant Thiang, in his last life as Mr. Poh, he was a cattle rustler who was caught stealing a cow. He was set upon by villagers who threw a knife into the back of his head and killed him. He then left his body, took rebirth as a ghost and thought of his beloved brother and went to him and saw his wife who was six months pregnant. He was drawn to her womb and somehow went inside, thus bumping out the previous being. This was the law of karma in action. He was close to his brother and her so his karma seems to have superseded the previous being. It's not that he consciously knew how to do this; he was just blown on by the winds of his karma. Sometimes pregnant women feel that something is wrong with the baby, and then it's all right again. It's possible that a being could die in the womb and leave, but the fetus is still usable so another spirit comes along and takes it over. These things do happen.

One example of a case suggestive of rebirth is that of Ratran Hami who was a man living in Sri Lanka in 1927. He got married to Podi Menike but still had to go to his wife's family to collect her. When he got there she had changed her mind and refused to go to his village with him. There was another man staying there who was Podhi Menike's mother's cousin and Ratran likely misinterpreted this and got jealous, thinking he was a rival. He was very offended and embarrassed by this so he went home, sharpened his Malay knife and went back and stabbed her to death. The people present jumped on Ratran and beat him and he was arrested. At his trial he said that he was set upon by these people and he acted in self defense but the stabbing was an accident. He was found guilty and sentenced to be hung.

Before he was hanged in July 1928 he told his brother that he would come back and he was thinking only of his brother at his hanging. They were both Theravadin Buddhists so they believed in rebirth. His brother remembered him saying that he would come back as his son. Then, more than 18 years later his brother was married and the couple had a baby boy with a stunted right arm with short knobby fingers webbed together and the major muscle of his right upper chest was missing. He surmised that his younger brother had returned to him but he never told his wife that he had a brother who was hanged for murder.

When the boy, Wijeratne was 2½ years old he began talking and brooding to himself about how he killed his wife, Podhi Menike in his past life which caused his malformed right arm. His mother listened to him and then told her husband about it but he was not surprised saying, "Oh honey, let me explain..." And he told her the whole story about his brother Ratran and Podhi Menike.

The boy went on to relate the important details of Ratran's life, including things that his father didn't know. For example he described that just before his hanging they tested the gallows by hanging a bag of sand. He described that after he was hanged he recalled falling into a pit of fire. Later he could recall flitting through the air from tree top to tree top, and once when he was in a state of delusion he acted out being a bird. This indicates that the karmic result of his act of murder may have been a temporary hellish rebirth followed by a rebirth as a bird. This is a very rare case of someone recalling an animal realm rebirth. His aspiration to return as his brother's son may have been important and helpful because he did succeed. The Buddha encouraged you to have an aspiration for where you would like to take rebirth and he describes this in the *Reappearance by Aspiration sutta in Middle Length Sayings No. 20* (Wisdom Publications). It's like your employer asking you, where do you see yourself five years from now?

Wijeratne completely confessed to the crime and said that he lied at his trial in his last life to get a reduced sentence. He was also unrepentant of his crime, saying that a man has a right to kill his wife if she refuses to go with him. After he grew up he was attracted to a girl who resembled Podi Menike in appearance and also in his perception that she was rejecting him. This triggered off a schizophrenic split within Wijeratne and Dr. Stevenson suggested that psychiatrists should realize that the cause of their patient's mental illness is sometimes traumas from their past lives. From a karmic perspective we can see that likely the reason why he couldn't have a good relationship with a woman is because he killed his wife in his past life. If he killed a soldier in battle, that would have been a different karma. By the time he reached age 35, he seems to have worked out his negative karma and he was married with two children, working as a school teacher and doing fine. By then he also changed his view and said that it would be best not to murder your wife in such a circumstance and it causes so much disruption for yourself and for both families involved.

Where Reincarnation and Biology Intersect is a landmark book by Dr. Ian Stevenson where he provides an overview of types of cases where birthmarks or other physiological manifestations have been found to relate to experiences of the remembered past life, particularly violent death. In chapter 6, "Birthmarks Corresponding to Wounds

Verified by Medical Records" he states that these cases "belong to the most important group in the entire collection. The medical records, usually postmortem reports, verify the correspondence between the birthmarks and the wounds with a certitude sometimes approached but never reached by the testimonies of informants drawing on their memories."

The first case is of Metin Koybasi. He could recall being a relative in his previous life named Hasim Koybasi who was shot in the head during the post election riot in the village in Turkey in 1963. Hasim was shot behind the left ear and the bullet was lodged on the front side of the front of the neck. The pathologist made a small incision and extracted the bullet. Metin had birthmarks on the back of the head and in the spot corresponding to the pathologists postmortem wound. He also had a powerful attitude of vengefulness toward the man who killed him in his previous life, as is often the situation in these cases. Metin once tried to take his father's gun and shoot this man, but was fortunately restrained. He later became more pacific.

There is a story from India of someone who was convicted of murder based on the testimony of their victim who was reborn and could later identify the killer. In another case, a boy told his father that in his previous life he was married and he hid some money in the wall of their home but didn't tell his wife. He needed to tell her so his father brought him to the house that he identified and they knocked on the door. Oh, excuse me but this is my son and he was your husband in his last life and he wants to show you where he hid some money? The little boy went straight to the spot and she found the money there! I don't know if she split some of the cash with him. Next, he forgot about his past life after he completed his mission.

In the courses I have been teaching on Buddhism since 1996 I have met many people with stories relating to past lives. One man told me that his father told him that when he was just two years old he told him that he was his father's father. His grandfather died two years before he was born so the timing fits. Another woman told my class that when she and her husband brought their six year old daughter to his parents' house for the first time in her life, she went upstairs to the bedroom and she remarked "Wow, this bedroom has changed a lot since I was here!" This indicates rebirth within families which is common enough. Another woman, with East Indian parents, clearly recalled that when she was three years old, and living in the Caribbean, she had a powerful experience that was like watching a movie film from her mind about a life as a man, over a century before, wearing a top hat and looking up to a balcony at a fair skinned woman whom he loved. When it was over she felt such an attachment to that lifetime that she cried and cried.

There are other categories of evidence for rebirth. One major area is past life regression hypnosis. This is a lot easier than the way the Buddha taught it. The Buddha taught the way to recall your previous lives but he said that you need to reach the third jhana. When you come out of it you avert your mind to your earliest memories, then go back further and further until you see your previous life. Jhana gives you such a clear mind that you can see such things. If it doesn't work you need to go into jhana again. Since the vast majority of people will never reach jhana in their entire lives, the easier way to recall your past existences is through a qualified hypnotherapist. I was adverse to this idea until I met Ajahn Brahm. I asked him about his knowledge of his previous lives and his experience with the jhanas but being a monk, his precepts don't allow him to tell lay people — only other monks. Being an ex-monk didn't help me. I was surprised to hear that Ajahn Brahm thought that past life regression could be helpful for people because if they have a vivid experience of an old man, with the certainty that it was them, then that would convince them of right view — karma and rebirth. He said you wouldn't just have to take rebirth just on faith; you would know for yourself. Now there's a good reason, because it helps establish you on the noble eightfold path.

I'm still skeptical, and for good reason, about a person's ability to dig up a past life in regression and the credibility of the hypnotist because they could give suggestions so all of this needs careful consideration when people claim to know their past lives. Some claims are untrue, however this has worked well for many people and I do recommend it. Peter Ramster, an Australian psychotherapist, has documented several thoroughly investigated cases. In his book *The Search for Lives Past* (Ramster 1990: 227) he cites the case of Cynthia Henderson, who "remembered a life during the French Revolution. When under trance, she spoke in French without any trace of an accent, understood and answered questions put to her in French, used dialect of the time, and knew the names of streets which had changed and were only discoverable on old maps".

One of the most incredible psychic phenomena, which religious people, skeptics and atheists have continuously and deliberately ignored is xenoglossy — the ability to speak or write a foreign language a person never learned. After all other explanations have been investigated — such as fraud, genetic memory, telepathy and cryptomnesia (the remembering of a foreign language learned earlier), xenoglossy is taken as evidence of *either* memories of a language learned in a past life *or* of communication with someone in the ghost realm. Dr. Ian Stevenson has done specialized research into xenoglossy and his book *Xenoglossy* (Stevenson 1974) is one of the leading scientific studies in this area. In it he documents a study he made of a 37 year old American woman. Under hypnosis she experienced a complete change of voice and personality into that of a male. She spoke fluently in the Swedish language—a language she did not speak or understand when in the normal state of consciousness. Another case he investigated involved an Indian woman named Uttar Huddar who at aged 32 spontaneously took on the personality of a housewife of West Bengal in the 1820s. She began speaking Bengali instead of her own language Marathi. For days or weeks at a time speakers of Bengali had to be brought in to enable her to communicate with her own family.

Another category of evidence is child prodigies who have developed certain skill sets in such a high degree in past lives that they become deeply ingrained in their persona. So when that person takes rebirth, the skills come along in the new body, fully intact and a child prodigy is born. For example, Wolfgang Amadeus Mozart believed that he had been a musician in many past lives where he had developed his amazing creative and technical skills.

One of the more surprising teachings of the Buddha is that it's hard not to meet people who, in the past were your mother or father, brother, sister, son, daughter or friend. You're bumping into them all the time because of the millions of combinations of past lives. So that is a bit about karma, its long time perspective and evidence for rebirth. Bhikkhu Bodhi's teachings are below. He is a senior American scholar monk who is known for his articulateness and orthodoxy.

Does Rebirth Make Sense?
by Venerable Bhikkhu Bodhi

Newcomers to Buddhism are usually impressed by the clarity, directness, and earthy practicality of the Dhamma as embodied in such basic teachings as the Four Noble Truths, the Noble Eightfold Path, and the threefold training. These teachings, as clear as daylight, are accessible to any serious seeker looking for a way beyond suffering. When, however, these seekers encounter the doctrine of rebirth, they often balk, convinced it just doesn't make sense. At this point, they suspect that the teaching has swerved off course, tumbling from the grand highway of reason into wistfulness and speculation. Even modernist interpreters of Buddhism seem to have trouble taking the rebirth teaching seriously. Some dismiss it as just a piece of cultural baggage, "ancient Indian metaphysics," that the Buddha retained in deference to the world view of his age. Others interpret it as a metaphor for the change of mental states, with the realms of rebirth seen as symbols for psychological archetypes. A few critics even question the authenticity of the texts on rebirth, arguing that they must be interpolations.

A quick glance at the Pali suttas would show that none of these claims has much substance. The teaching of rebirth crops up almost everywhere in the Canon, and is so closely bound to a host of other doctrines that to remove it would virtually reduce the Dhamma to tatters. Moreover, when the suttas speak about rebirth into the five realms — the hells, the animal world, the spirit realm, the human world, and the heavens — they never hint that these terms are meant symbolically. To the contrary, they even say that rebirth occurs "with the breakup of the body, after death," which clearly implies they intend the idea of rebirth to be taken quite literally.

In this essay I won't be arguing the case for the scientific validity of rebirth. Instead, I wish to show that the idea of rebirth makes sense. I will be contending that it "makes sense" in two ways: first, in that it is intelligible, having meaning both intrinsically and in relation to the Dhamma as a whole; and second, in that it helps us "to make sense," to understand our own place in the world. I will try to establish this in relation to three domains of discourse, the ethical, the ontological, and the soteriological. Don't be frightened by the big words: the meaning will become clear as we go along.

I

First, the teaching of rebirth makes sense *in relation to ethics.* For early Buddhism, the conception of rebirth is an essential plank of its ethical theory, providing an incentive for avoiding evil and doing good. In this context, the doctrine of rebirth is correlated with the principle of kamma, which asserts that all our morally determinate actions, our wholesome and unwholesome deeds, have an inherent power to bring forth fruits that correspond to the moral quality of those deeds. Taken together, the twin teachings of rebirth and kamma show that a principle of moral equilibrium obtains between our actions and the felt quality of our lives, such that morally good deeds produce agreeable results, bad deeds disagreeable results.

It is only too obvious that such moral equilibrium cannot be found within the limits of a single life. We can observe, often poignantly, that morally unscrupulous people might enjoy happiness, esteem, and success, while people who lead lives of the highest integrity are bowed down beneath pain and misery. For the principle of moral equilibrium to work, some type of survival beyond the present life is required, for kamma can bring its due retribution only if our individual "streams of consciousness" do not terminate with death. Two different forms of survival are possible: on the one hand, an eternal afterlife in heaven or hell, on the other a sequence of rebirths. Of these alternatives, the hypothesis of rebirth seems far more compatible with moral justice than an eternal afterlife; for any finite good action, it seems, must eventually exhaust its potency, and no finite bad action, no matter how bad, should warrant eternal damnation.

It may be the case that this insistence on some kind of moral equity is an illusion, an unrealistic demand we superimpose on a universe cold and indifferent to our hopes. There is no logical way to *prove* the validity of rebirth and kamma. The naturalist might just be right in holding that personal existence comes to an end at death, and with it all prospects for moral justice. Nevertheless, I believe such a thesis flies in the face of one of our deepest moral intuitions, a sense that some kind of moral justice must ultimately prevail. To show that this is so, let us consider two limiting cases of ethically decisive action. As the limiting case of immoral action, let us take Hitler, who was directly responsible for the dehumanizing deaths of perhaps ten million people. As the limiting case of moral action, let us consider a man who sacrifices his own life to save the lives of total strangers. Now if there is no survival beyond death, both men reap the same ultimate destiny. Before dying, perhaps, Hitler experiences some pangs of despair; the self-sacrificing hero enjoys a few seconds of satisfaction knowing he's performing a noble deed. Then beyond that — there is nothing, except in others' memories. Both are obliterated, reduced to lifeless flesh and bones.

Now the naturalist might be correct in drawing this conclusion, and in holding that those who believe in survival and retribution are just projecting their own wishes out upon the world. But I think something within us resists consigning both Hitler and our compassionate hero to the same fate. The reason we resist is because we have a deep intuitive sense that a principle of moral justice is at work in the world, regulating the course of events in such a way that our good and bad actions rebound upon ourselves to bring the appropriate fruit. Where the naturalist holds that this intuition amounts to nothing more than a projection of our own ideals out upon the world, I would contend that the very fact that we can conceive a demand for moral justice has a significance that is more than merely psychological. However vaguely, our subjective sense of moral justice reflects an objective reality, a principle of moral equilibrium that is not mere projection but is built into the very bedrock of actuality.

The above considerations are not intended to make belief in rebirth a necessary basis for ethics. The Buddha himself does not try to found ethics on the ideas of kamma and rebirth, but uses a purely naturalistic type of moral reasoning that does not presuppose personal survival or the working of kamma. The gist of his reasoning is simply that we should not mistreat others — by injuring them, stealing their belongings, exploiting them sexually, or deceiving them — because we ourselves are averse to being treated in such ways. Nevertheless, though the Buddha does not found ethics on the theory of rebirth, he does make belief in kamma and rebirth a strong inducement to moral behavior. When we recognize that our good and bad actions can rebound upon ourselves, determining our future lives and bringing us happiness or suffering, this gives us a decisive reason to avoid unwholesome conduct and to diligently pursue the good.

The Buddha includes belief in rebirth and kamma in his definition of right view, and their explicit denial in wrong view. It is not that the desire for the fruits of good karma should be one's main motive for leading a moral life, but rather that acceptance of these teachings inspires and reinforces our commitment to ethical ideals. These twin principles open a window to a wider background against which our pursuit of the moral life unfolds. They show us that our present living conditions, our dispositions and aptitudes, our virtues and faults, result from our actions in previous lives. When we realize that our present conditions reflect our kammic past, we will also realize that our present actions are the legacy that we will transmit to our kammic descendants, that is, to ourselves in future lives. The teaching of rebirth thus enables us to face the future with fortitude, dignity, and courage. If we recognize that no matter how debilitating our present conditions might be, no matter how limiting and degrading, we can still redeem ourselves, we will be spurred to exercise our will for the achievement of our future good. By our present actions of body, speech, and mind, we can transform ourselves, and by transforming ourselves, we can surmount all inner and outer obstacles and advance toward the final goal.

The teachings of kamma and rebirth have a still deeper ethical significance than as simple pointers to moral responsibility. They show us not only that our personal lives are shaped by our own kammic past, but also that we live in an ethically meaningful universe. Taken in conjunction, they make the universe a *cosmos*, an orderly, integrated whole, with dimensions of significance that transcend the merely physical. The levels of order that we

A Short Walk On An Ancient Path

have access to by direct inspection or scientific investigation do not exhaust all the levels of cosmic order. There is system and pattern, not only in the physical and biological domains, but also in the ethical, and the teachings of kamma and rebirth reveal just what that pattern is. Although this ethical order is invisible to our fleshly eyes and cannot be detected by scientific apparatus, this does not mean it is not real. Beyond the range of normal perception, a moral law holds sway over our deeds and, via our deeds, over our destiny. It is just the principle of kamma, operating across the sequence of rebirths, that locks our volitional actions into the dynamics of the cosmos, thus making ethics an expression of the cosmos's own intrinsic orderliness.

II

The teaching of rebirth, taken in conjunction with the doctrine of kamma, implies that we live in a morally ordered universe, one in which our morally determinate actions bring forth fruits that in some way correspond to their own ethical quality. Though the moral law that links our actions with their fruits cannot be demonstrated experimentally in the same way that physical and chemical laws can be, this does not mean it is not real. It means only that, like quarks and quasars, it operates beyond the threshold of sensory perception. Far from being a mere projection of our subjective ideals, the moral law locks our volitional deeds into an all-embracing cosmic order that is perfectly objective in that it functions independently of our personal desires, views, and beliefs. Thus when we submit our behavior to the rule of ethics, we are not simply acting in ways that merit moral approval. By conforming to the principles of ethics we are doing nothing less than aligning ourselves with the Dhamma, the universal law of righteousness and truth which stands at the bedrock of the cosmos.

This brings us to the ontological aspect of the Buddhist teaching on rebirth, its implications for understanding the nature of being. Buddhism sees the process of rebirth as integral to the principle of conditionality that runs through all existence. The sentient universe is regulated by different orders of causation layered in such a way that higher orders of causation can exercise dominion over lower ones. The order of kamma, which governs the process of rebirth, is a higher order of causation, and at some level, not within the range of investigation by ordinary empirical means, it intersects with the lower orders of physical and biological causation, bending their energies toward the fulfillment of its own potential. The Buddha does not posit a divine judge who rules over the workings of kamma, rewarding and punishing us for our deeds. The kammic process functions autonomously, without a supervisor or director, entirely through the intrinsic power of volitional action. Interwoven with other orders in the vast, complex web of conditionality, our deeds produce their consequences just as naturally as seeds in a field bring forth their appropriate herbs and flowers.

To understand how kamma can produce its effects across the succession of rebirths we must invert our normal, everyday conception of the relationship between consciousness and matter. Under the influence of materialistic biases we assume that material existence is determinative of consciousness. Because we witness bodies being born into this world and observe how the mind matures in tandem with the body, we tacitly take the body to be the foundation of our existence and mind or consciousness an evolutionary offshoot of blind material processes. Matter wins the honored status of "objective reality," and mind becomes an accidental intruder upon an inherently senseless universe.

From the Buddhist perspective, however, consciousness and the world coexist in a relationship of mutual creation which equally requires both terms. Just as there can be no consciousness without a body to serve as its physical support and a world as its sphere of cognition, so there can be no physical organism and no world without some type of consciousness to constitute them as an organism and world. Though temporally neither mind nor matter can be regarded as prior to the other, in terms of practical importance the Buddha says that mind is the forerunner. Mind is the forerunner, not in the sense that it arises before the body or can exist independently of a physical medium, but in the sense that the body and the world in which we find ourselves reflect our mental activity.

It is mental activity, in the form of volition, that constitutes kamma, and it is our stock of kamma that steers the stream of consciousness from the past life into a new body. Thus the Buddha says: "This body, O monks, is old kamma, to be seen as generated and fashioned by volition, as something to be felt" (SN XI.37). It is not only the body, as a composite whole, that is the product of past kamma, but the sense faculties too (see SN XXV.146). The eye, ear, nose, tongue, body-sense, and mind-base are also fashioned by our past kamma, and thus kamma to some degree shapes and influences all our sensory experience. Since kamma is ultimately explained

A Short Walk On An Ancient Path

as volition (*cetana*), this means that the particular body with which we are endowed, with all its distinguishing features and faculties of sense, is rooted in our volitional activities in earlier lives. Precisely how past volition can influence the development of the zygote lies beyond the range of scientific explanation, but if the Buddha's words are to be trusted such an influence must be real.

The channel for the transmission of kammic influence from life to life across the sequence of rebirths is the individual stream of consciousness. Consciousness embraces both phases of our being — that in which we generate fresh kamma and that in which we reap the fruits of old kamma — and thus in the process of rebirth, consciousness bridges the old and new existences. Consciousness is not a single transmigrating entity, a self or soul, but a stream of evanescent acts of consciousness, each of which arises, briefly subsists, and then passes away. This entire stream, however, though made up of evanescent units, is fused into a unified whole by the causal relations obtaining between all the occasions of consciousness in any individual continuum. At a deep level, each occasion of consciousness inherits from its predecessor the entire kammic legacy of that particular stream; in perishing, it in turn passes that content on to its successor, increased by its own novel contribution. Thus our volitional deeds do not exhaust their full potential in their immediately visible effects. Every volitional deed that we perform, when it passes, leaves behind a subtle imprint stamped upon the onward-flowing stream of consciousness. The deed deposits in the stream of consciousness a seed capable of bearing fruit, of producing a result that matches the ethical quality of the deed.

When we encounter suitable external conditions, the kammic seeds deposited in our mental continuum rise up from their dormant condition and produce their fruits. The most important function performed by kamma is to generate rebirth into an appropriate realm, a realm that provides a field for it to unfold its stored potentials. The bridge between the old existence and the new is, as we said above, the evolving stream of consciousness. It is within this stream of consciousness that the kamma has been created through the exercise of volition; it is this same stream of consciousness, flowing on, that carries the kammic energies into the new existence; and it is again this same stream of consciousness that experiences the fruit. Conceivably, at the deepest level all the individual streams of consciousness are integrated into a single all-embracing matrix, so that, beneath the surface of events, the separate kammic accumulations of all living beings crisscross, overlap, and merge. This hypothesis — though speculative — would help account for the strange coincidences we sometimes meet that prick holes in our assumptions of rational order.

The generative function of kamma in the production of new existence is described by the Buddha in a short but pithy sutta preserved in the Anguttara Nikaya (AN III.76). Venerable Ananda approaches the Master and says, "'Existence, existence' is spoken of, venerable sir. In what way is there existence?" The Buddha replies: "If there were no kamma ripening in the sensory realm, no sense-sphere existence would be discerned. If there where no kamma ripening in the form realm, no form-sphere existence would be discerned. If there were no kamma ripening in the formless realm, no formless-sphere existence would be discerned. Therefore, Ananda, kamma is the field, consciousness the seed, and craving the moisture for beings obstructed by ignorance and fettered by craving to be established in a new realm of existence, either low (sense-sphere), middling (form-sphere), or high (formless-sphere)."

As long as ignorance and craving, the twin roots of the round of rebirths, remain intact in our mental continuum, at the time of death one especially powerful kamma will become ascendant and propel the stream of consciousness to the realm of existence that corresponds to its own "vibrational frequency." When consciousness, as the seed, becomes planted or "established" in that realm it sprouts forth into the rest of the psycho-physical organism, summed up in the expression "name and form" (nama-rupa). As the organism matures, it provides the site for other past kammas to gain the opportunity to produce their results. Then, within this new existence, in response to our various kammically induced experiences, we engage in actions that engender fresh kamma with the capacity to generate still another rebirth. Thereby the round of existence keeps turning from one life to the next, as the stream of consciousness, swept along by craving and steered by kamma, assumes successive modes of embodiment.

The ultimate implication of the Buddha's teaching on kamma and rebirth is that human beings are the final masters of their own destiny. Through our unwholesome deeds, rooted in greed, hatred, and delusion, we create unwholesome kamma, the generative cause of bad rebirths, of future misery and bondage. Through our wholesome deeds, rooted in generosity, kindness, and wisdom, we beautify our minds and thereby create kamma productive of a happy rebirth. By using wisdom to dig more deeply below the superficial face of things, we can uncover the subtle truths hidden by our preoccupation with appearances. Thereby we can uproot the binding defilements and win the peace of deliverance, the freedom beyond the cycle of kamma and its fruit.

III

The third way in which the teaching on rebirth makes sense is the soteriological, a word which means "in relation to final liberation." According to the Buddha's teaching, a doctrine of rebirth is not only possible but also necessary because the goal of the teaching is nothing short of liberation from samsara, the round of rebirths. It was dismay at the prospect of endless rebirths, each terminating in old age, sickness, and death, that drove the young prince Siddhattha out from the luxurious life of the palace into the forest as an earnest, homeless mendicant seeking the path to enlightenment: "Being myself subject to birth, old age, sickness, and death, I went forth seeking the birthless, ageless, illness-free, deathless Nibbana, the supreme security from bondage" (MN 26.12). His attainment of enlightenment marked not merely the realization of a state of wisdom and inward peace, but the conviction that he had brought the beginningless round of rebirths to an end: "This is my last birth. There is now for me no renewal of existence" (MN 26.18). When he went out to teach the Dhamma, his purpose was to guide others to the same state of release that he himself had won. Again, this release was not merely relief from psychological suffering, from pain and distress. It was release from the round of becoming, which means from the round of rebirths. When his first five disciples, the "bhikkhus of the group of five," learned the Dhamma from him and brought their practice to fulfillment, they too were able to confirm: "This is our last birth. There is now for us no renewal of existence" (MN 26.30). And as the Buddha's Teaching spread, many young men and women went forth from the household life into homelessness in order to find a way out from the sea of endless birth and death, which is the sea of suffering.

Any religion flourishes against the background of a particular culture and acquires meaning from the concepts prevalent in that culture. Since different epochs and cultures are governed by different conceptual frameworks, different "paradigms," one might say that a particular religion or spiritual teaching has to be explained in terms of the conceptual framework prevailing in the culture in which it has taken root. This would apply to Buddhism as much as to any other religion, perhaps even more so because of its freedom from rigid dogma. Thus, one might argue, the Buddha expounded the Dhamma against the background of the Indian belief systems of his day, in which the idea of rebirth was generally taken for granted. In our own time such concepts as rebirth and kamma are either alien (as in the West) or outdated (for those in the East who adopt modern Western modes of thought). So, it might be asked, can't we preserve the essence of the Buddha's teaching as a practical, therapeutic path to liberation from suffering without bringing along the extra cultural baggage passed down from bygone centuries, namely, the idea that equates liberation from suffering with liberation from rebirth? Surely such basic Buddhist teachings as the Four Noble Truths, dependent origination, and the three characteristics are all meaningful apart from the doctrine of rebirth. Surely one can practice the Noble Eightfold Path without believing that one's practice is going to release one from the prospects of coming back to life in this world or any other world.

The reply I would give to this proposal is a twofold one: first, I would say that if one doubts the teaching of rebirth but still recognizes the validity of such basic Buddhist teachings as the Four Noble Truths, and if one personally benefits from Buddhist practices, one should certainly adopt Buddhist teachings and practices in whatever way one wishes. If one follows these teachings sincerely, without misrepresenting them, they are bound to confer blessings on one's own life and on the lives of those within one's sphere of influence. But, I would continue, this is quite another matter from saying that we can revise the Buddha's Teaching without diluting it; that we can divest the Buddha's Teaching of the concept of rebirth without diminishing its depth and meaning. Even such fundamental teachings as the Four Noble Truths and dependent origination, if studied closely, will be seen to be intimately connected to the idea of rebirth; for the very idea of suffering or *dukkha* central to both these teachings gains a fuller meaning only when it is recognized to be the suffering of repeated birth. This point has been eloquently explained by Ven. Nyanatiloka Mahathera in his classic *The Word of the Buddha:*

A Short Walk On An Ancient Path

Samsara — the wheel of existence, lit. the "perpetual wander-
ing" — is the name given in the Pali scriptures to the sea of life
ever restlessly heaving up and down, the symbol of this con-
tinuous process of ever again and again being born, growing
old, suffering, and dying…. Of this samsara, a single lifetime
constitutes only a tiny fraction. Hence, to be able to compre-
hend the first noble truth, one must let one's gaze rest upon
the samsara, upon this frightful sequence of rebirths, and not
merely upon one single lifetime, which, of course, may some-
times be not very painful.

(Nyanatiloka Mahathera, *The Word of the Buddha,* 17th edition. Kandy:
Buddhist Publication Society, 2001, p. 18)

The concept of rebirth relates to the quest for liberation not only in setting
the problem with which the Buddha's teaching deals but also in providing
the condition needed for the realization of its final goal. That is, rebirth is
not only that from which we must attain release; perhaps paradoxically, it
is also that which makes release possible. What I mean by this seeming
paradox is that the final goal of the Dhamma, liberation, is achieved by
perfecting certain spiritual qualities, above all the "five spiritual faculties" of
faith, energy, mindfulness, concentration, and wisdom, and other spiritual
virtues like generosity, moral discipline, patience, truthfulness, loving-
kindness, and equanimity, which for most people require many lives to
reach maturity. There may be a few people in whom these qualities are so
prominent that they can be confident of attaining the final goal within this
life itself — perhaps there are even a few who have already attained it—but
for most, the requisite qualities still need further maturation before realization of the final goal becomes a realistic prospect. These faculties have to
be "ripened" until they are strong and sharp enough to make the breakthrough to world-transcending liberation, and this requires time; in most
cases, it requires long periods of time, much longer than a single lifetime.

When we reflect upon the degree to which such qualities as mindfulness,
concentration, and wisdom had been developed by the noble ones of the
past, and the degree to which we ourselves have developed them, we
will see that a great distance separates us from their attainments. This
should not be a cause for dejection or despair; but it is a reminder of the
immense amount of work we must do on ourselves to reach the plane

of the noble ones. Now as we strive to practice the Dhamma within this life, we receive a certain amount of "immediate returns" in the form of the greater peace and happiness to which the practice leads. But we also understand that this is not itself the final goal. This is not the great realization that the noble ones celebrate when they utter their lion's roar. What gives us the confidence that the practices we undertake now, in this present life, are contributing to our ultimate attainment of liberation is our trust in the principle of rebirth. It is the fact that life — or more precisely, the "stream of consciousness" — does not end with our bodily death that assures us that the wholesome qualities we cultivate in this present life are preserved and consolidated within the ongoing sequence of lives that constitutes our individual identity through samsara. From life to life, the body dies, the stream of consciousness constantly changes; it is not an immortal, changeless self. Yet while our good and bad deeds bring their desired and undesired fruits, our wholesome qualities, guided by the Dhamma, governed by the Dhamma, also acquire momentum. Like a snowball rolling down the side of a mountain, which accumulates more and more snow until it sets off an avalanche, our wholesome qualities, our spiritual faculties, gain an energy of their own, which builds up from one life to the next, as long as we continue to practice the Dhamma, until they gain sufficient momentum to break the downward "gravitational pull" of the defilements, of ignorance and craving, of greed, hatred, and delusion. It is then that we can make the breakthrough to liberation, stage by stage, and when we reach the final stage, we end the round of rebirths.

We can thus see that, in relation to the quest for liberation, the state of bondage from which liberation is sought and the ground that makes liberation possible are the same. The state of bondage is the round of rebirths: a condition of suffering marked by aging, sickness, and death which we undergo over and over as long as we are in the grip of ignorance and craving. But while the deluded, ordinary person without access to the Dhamma remains in bondage to this round of rebirths, those who encounter the Dhamma find the path that leads to final liberation, to the unconditioned peace and freedom of Nibbana. Only the noble ones — those who have reached stream-entry and the higher stages — are assured that they will win the final goal. But those who place trust in the Dhamma and earnestly endeavor to cultivate the path can gradually advance towards the ultimate goal. Since only a few will consummate their endeavors in this lifetime, for the others, the process of rebirth becomes a process that enables them to sharpen and strengthen their spiritual faculties. Each successive life guided by the Dhamma preserves the achievements of earlier lives, providing a base from which we can continue our efforts to develop our virtues, purify our minds, and deepen our wisdom. When our moral discipline, concentration, and wisdom reach their culmination, we come to the end of the round of rebirths. However, we could never have reached that goal if there were not a series of rebirths through which our spiritual virtues could have been broadened and deepened.

Shrine on the water, Thailand

Karma and Rebirth

Thai lady dressed as a deva

Chapter 5

Buddhist Cosmology

*"When one does not understand death,
life can be very confusing."*
Ajahn Chah

"God is Dead," read the headlines on the *New York Times* on a Christmas day, as in the Elton John song from the 1970s. Literally speaking, the New York Times wasn't quite right but the truth is something else. Cosmology is defined as the theory or philosophy of the nature and principles of the universe. There is no God in Buddhism because the highest state attainable is nibbana and nibbana is not personal. God usually means a personal being but the Buddha has, roughly speaking, merged with nibbana. Nibbana is like an element. Buddhists don't feel that they can pray to the Buddha. We're not talking to him and he's not listening to us. We have his teachings to put into practice but there's a big difference here from the theistic religions. The Buddha wasn't interested in the idea of God and he didn't think that believing in God was useful to help people overcome attachment. But Buddhism provides a detailed cosmology with 31 planes of existence. There are higher realm beings and the law of karma and rebirth acts upon us all so there's no need for a God.

Beyond the physical universe, described at the end of this chapter, the Buddha explained the dharma of the unseen dimensions, or realms of existence. This explains a lot of things in the world and in your own inner and past life. Let's take a look at these realms of existence. There are five realms of existence, two higher realms and three lower realms. The Buddha taught that every sentient being in the universe lives in one of these five realms. This is samsara, the wheel of life, the continual running on from life to life, like a monkey who jumps from tree to tree never finding fruit. The characteristics of samsara are continuous struggle, fear of death, ignorance of birth, and the repetition of that struggle.

It may be helpful to relate to the realms as states of mind because the dominant reason for rebirth always lies in the mind. The Buddha says that mind is the architect of the whole universe. On any one day you may go through each and every realm as a state of mind. The hell realm is characterized as constant anger and aggression. You get angry at people and they respond with anger at you. This makes you more angry at them so they get even more angry at you. This vicious circle becomes a living hell. The animal realm is characterized by ignorance and strong brutish desires with blind lust, or dull stupidity. The symbol is a pig. A pig just eats everything in front of its nose, not looking right, not looking left. He doesn't care if he's eating garbage or caviar or chocolates, he just stubbornly eats and eats and eats. Ignorance means not paying attention to the signals that life is giving you, being stuck on your habitual patterns, too comfortable and cozy with your old way of doing things. Such people can be quite intelligent in their ignorance. They think of clever ways to convince you to adopt their habitual patterns. "You should come to the pub with us after work. Why spend your time on meditation. A bit of alcohol is good for your health." There is also the absence of a sense of humour because animals cannot appreciate irony. The comfort zone is the single biggest enemy of human potential. The tendency to stay with what is comfortable is the animal realm mentality. There's no challenge to it. Oscar Wilde said, "Only the shallow know themselves."

The hungry ghost realm is one of poverty mentality, selfishness, possessiveness and intense clinging. You can't get enough money, you can't get enough food, you can't get enough love or attention, or stamps for your stamp collection. Even if you get what you want, it's as though you've fallen in love with being hungry and you would rather still be hungry. The symbol of the ghost realm is of a ghost, which is an afflicted spirit, with a pinprick mouth, a long skinny neck and a huge ravenous belly that is always hungry. No matter how fast he eats, 24 hours a day, he can never be satisfied.

In the higher realms, the dominant forces in our minds will be human states, states tied to the human world. This is the basic tone of our consciousness. The human realm state of mind is characterized by passion, discriminating passion. You want your coffee a certain way with cream, not milk, and just a little bit of sugar. You're very particular about the clothes you wear. Humans want to do more, have more and be more. Their ego strives for growth and expansion. That's discriminating passion. Animals don't have that. Once they satisfy their needs to eat, sleep and procreate, they just lie down and sleep and/or die. Cats sleep 15 hours a day.

The god realm is characterized by bliss, a blissed-out state of mind, where everything seems beautiful and wonderful but it is an impermanent state of mind. Bhikkhu Bodhi said (Bodhi 1984) "At times very noble thoughts will arise in us, making us feel divine or heavenly, thoughts such as supreme generosity, great kindness and compassion. With such thoughts, our world becomes very light and pure, almost like a heavenly world. These states of mind are, in fact, the seeds for rebirth in the heavenly worlds."

The jealous god mind set is a paranoid state of mind, with greed for power, jealousy and envy, competitiveness, the urge for power with the paranoia of competitive higher beings that do not want anyone to be better than them. Vice-president Lyndon Johnson is an example of the asura, jealous god mentality. He was well known for his huge ego and he had a maniacal desire to be president. I have seen enough evidence, and I invite you to check it, to believe that he conspired to kill John F. Kennedy so that he could fulfill his power craving to be the President of the United States. Some of the same members of the FBI, like J. Edgar Hoover and the CIA, who helped Johnson with that murder were also part of the later assassination of Bobby Kennedy, but I haven't seen enough evidence yet to prove that Johnson initiated that assassination too. The jealous gods, called the asuras in Pali, just cannot bear to witness devas of more virtue so they attack them but the jealous gods always lose in the end.

The five realms in the wheel of life are illustrated below.

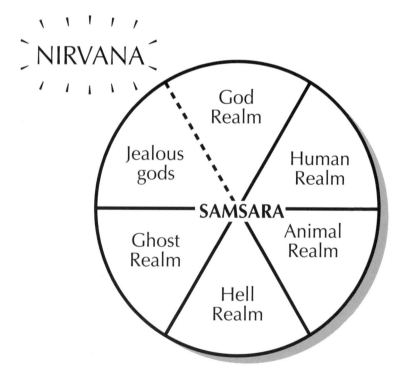

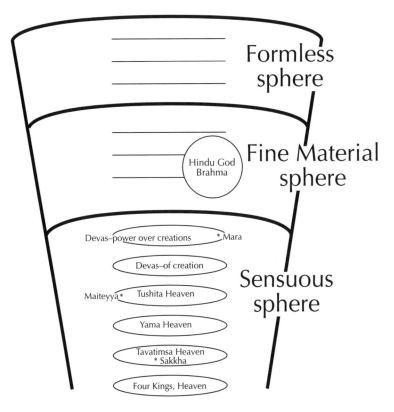

Formless sphere

Fine Material sphere

Hindu God Brahma

Devas–power over creations   * Mara

Devas–of creation

Maiteyya*   Tushita Heaven

Sensuous sphere

Yama Heaven

Tavatimsa Heaven
* Sakkha

Four Kings, Heaven

Above is an enlargement of the god realm as described in the suttas.
The six lower heavens of the sensuous sphere have a hierarchy to them
and are all occupied by devas which include the jealous gods or asuras.
The asuras are often depicted as a sixth realm — the jealous god realm,
but the Buddha described the asuras as a type of deva and a lower
deva, so they live together with the devas and particularly in the
second heaven, Tavatimsa.

Having considered the five realms as states of mind, next, contemplate the literal words of the Buddha that these are genuine realms,
like dimensions, where real beings actually live. The animal realm
and the human realm are the only ones you can see with the naked
eye. But if someone had a radio that could only pick up two stations,

he may say that his radio gets all the radio stations in town, but that isn't true. Because of the lower concentration of our minds, we do not, normally, have the mental energy to sense the other three realms. The word concentration is synonymous with energy. The Buddha saw all realms and he described them in great detail for us.

The god realm is divided into the sensuous sphere, the fine material sphere or Brahma world (Brahmaloka), and the immaterial or formless sphere. See the illustration. The sensuous sphere is comprised of six lower heavens. In the Theravada canon, the Buddha expounded at length on the nature of each of these six heavens. Western Buddhists generally have little idea about this, but the Buddha felt that it was important for him to tell us all about these things that ordinary worldlings cannot perceive. Practically every third sutta has devas involved. They're referred to numerous times in the scriptures.

Because many Westerners regard Buddhism as meditation, they generally have a lopsided view of what the Buddha taught. At Douglas College, I discussed the topic of devas with philosophy professor Leonard Angel and he believed that the Buddha was being metaphorical in referring to devas. Perhaps the Buddha was being polite to the pre-Hindu beliefs of the day, and maybe devas don't really exist at all, he felt. Dr. Angel practices Zen and he tries to synthesize modern scientific ideas with the enlightenment quest in his book *Enlightenment East & West*. I cannot accept his view because the pre-Hindus didn't all believe in devas. They had all kinds of conflicting views. And I find the belief that devas don't exist, is more unbelievable than the view that devas do exist. Consider the big picture of death, rebirth, karma, and the realms of existence. If devas don't exist, which is to say that the god realm does not exist and there is no heaven, then what happens to virtuous people after they die? If they come back to human birth and if people believe that, then why is it unbelievable that they could take rebirth as a deva in the god realm? It is an accounting nightmare to try to erase any one of the realms. The law of karma is the law of karma. We have to have these various destinations in order for the whole universe to hang together properly.

Practically all religions have devas. They indirectly confirm each other and the truth that there really is some objective reality which is reflected in all of these similar religious views. This isn't just the wishful thinking of people who want to live after death. Guardian angels, heavenly hosts, ascended masters, guides, spirit guides — they're all names for devas. Devas are not enlightened as a rule, and humans are not enlightened as a rule, but like humans it is still possible for a deva to attain to full and complete enlightenment. There are many cases of this in the suttas.

The first heaven of the sensuous sphere is ruled over by four principal devas. They are called the Four Great Kings — of the north, south, east and west but really these are psychological directions, useful for memory. Amongst the devas of the east are the gandharbas, kind of musical devas. In the south are the kumbhandas who can be tricksters, which may indicate that the Irish leprechaun may exist. In the west are nagas which are the serpent, snake or dragon kind of devas which you see commonly in Asian art and in depictions protecting the Buddha. Nagas have the ability to take on human form and the suttas describe a naga who was devoted to the Buddha so he took on the form of a man and was ordained as a monk; but one day he fell asleep in the temple which caused him to go back to his naga form. The other monks then told him he had to disrobe, because he wasn't really human. Because of this incident, during ordination ceremonies a monk is asked if he is a human being. Nagas like the water. This is a Buddhist explanation of what the Lock Ness Monster is. Thousands of nagas have been reported in lakes in China over the centuries. You can look up accounts in the West from the 16th century to World War One, of European sailors on ships who saw sea serpents, which are nagas, over the entire Atlantic Ocean. They were described in much the same way, by people from different countries who had no connection to each other. Accounts say they had a head like a cow or a dog or were flat shaped with eyes on the top like a frog. They resembled snakes and sometimes raised their head six feet out of the water, their bodies curved and had scales. It was believed to be a very bad omen to fire upon one because as a consequence, your ship might never reach port.

The nagas are sometimes in conflict with garudas, who are a type of a god realm bird, just as birds sometimes attack snakes. This first heaven is the realm of flying things and a Buddhist theory about UFOs is that some of them could be devas. In the Atanata sutta, the Buddha says "Cars fit for gods they have as well," and then he goes on to describe deva cities in this first, lowest heaven. "Gods" means the devas and "cars" refers to the vehicles that the devas cruise around in. Distinguishing them is this way could be interpreted as one type of UFO.

In the north reside the yakkhas. A yakkha is lower than a deva but it's not a ghost. It is an inter-dimensional being. The Sanskrit translation is yakshas, which sounds closer to the native Indian name sasquatch, which is just what it is. This is the Bigfoot. The Buddha actually had discourses with Yakkhas. Yakkhas are described just like the Bigfoot — tall, hairy and repulsively smelly. These are important ancient teachings which can help us to understand the Bigfoot mystery today and there is good evidence that Buddhist monks came by boat to the west coast of Canada and the U.S. as early as the 5th century AD. They may have influenced such native Indian beliefs, as the sasquatch. Many native Indians believe in rebirth, which may indicate a forgotten Buddhist influence.

There's even an explanation about why no one ever finds the body of a sasquatch. The reason is given in *The Questions of King Milinda* which is a book from three centuries after the Buddha when a Greek King in India named Milinda puts questions to the arahant Nigasena. He asked the arahant why is it that no remains of a Yakkha are ever found. Do such beings exist? Oh yes, Nigasena replied, such beings do indeed exist but their remains are not recognized as remains. Their remains look like sticks and stones and ants and scorpions and insects. This is because they are an inter-dimensional being. They phase into our world from another realm, we see them for a while, then they phase out. They are not a part human, part ape species that has descended over a long period of time so that's why people can't capture them or get enough evidence to convince others that they even exist: but they do exist.

Their behaviour is problematic. Yakkhas are like gangs that go around and make trouble. The Buddha said "People will not believe how many people have been killed by yakkhas," but they are not all bad. The Buddha once met with two yakkhas who were each the leader of a company of 500 yakkhas, who were also present. The Buddha gave them all a deep dhamma discourse as they all had the ability to comprehend it. At the end of his discourse all 1000 yakkhas transformed into beautiful devas and they attained the first stage of enlightenment, stream entry.

Moving upstairs, the second heaven is Tavatimsa heaven which is ruled over by Sakka, 'king of the gods', as he is called. This heaven is higher than the first one. The Buddha told a story about an ordinary king who had a virtuous minister. The minister was a very compassionate man and he helped many people. They both died and went to heaven. The king took rebirth as a deva in the first heaven. He lived in a celestial palace but it was rather dull and unexciting. He could perceive that his former minister took rebirth as a deva in Tavatimsa heaven. He objected, thinking "Hey! I was the king. How come I'm stuck here in this boring heaven while my minister gets a better rebirth up there in Tavatimsa heaven?" Then, he realized that he wasn't that generous or caring as a king, so the minister deserved a better rebirth than he did. This story illustrates the difference between these two heavens.

The second heaven is more often mentioned by the Buddha than any other heaven, perhaps because it is closer to Earth and our worldly affairs than the higher heavens. Sakka came down many times to visit the Buddha and he is referred to more than any other deva in the scriptures, including Brahma. Sakka rules in a celestial palace with thirty three principal devas in his administration. This heaven is called the gods of the thirty-three. When Buddhists say 'gods' they mean devas. Sakka was very virtuous when he was a human being so because of that, he took rebirth as Sakka. He has great goodness and virtue in character but he's not the smartest, you might say. Sakka rules for his lifetime which is generally one kalpa long, so he has a temporary administration like the President of the United States. After he dies and takes rebirth elsewhere, another Sakka will come along to replace him. Life in all five realms is impermanent. The Jataka Tales, the 572 past life stories attributed to the Buddha, are full of the heroic deeds of Sakka appearing in the sky above the Earth with great brilliance, to save the lives of a hero or heroine being picked on by some wicked king or other.

In Sanskrit, 'Sakka' translates as 'Indra,' which is a more familiar name to people. The existence of this Hindu god was confirmed by the Buddha. The Buddha's cousin and senior disciple Anuruddha was Sakka in a previous life and Anuruddha had the noble bearing of a king. Tavatimsa is like an endless garden party that goes on for a century with nothing going wrong. Not a bad choice for rebirth, eh? The jealous god devas are mixed together with the good devas in Tavatimsa heaven and they have their cosmic battles going on. Sakka once paid homage to the Buddha by saying to the Buddha that when they have wars with the asuras, they drink asura nectar, but the taste is not one sixteenth as sweet as the taste of the Buddha's dharma. This conjures up images of vast cosmological battles going on in the upstairs above our heads. This is actually the truth. This is what is really happening above us but we can't see it. It's like the titans in Greek cosmology, fighting it out with the gods.

Shortly after enlightenment, the Buddha spent one rainy season retreat in Tavatimsa Heaven teaching the dharma to his mother and to the millions of devas present. Nice son. The Buddha's mother died a week after Prince Siddhartha was born. This is the tradition for the mothers of the Buddhas of the past and the mothers of the Buddhas of the future. Queen Mahamaya was a deva in Tushita heaven but repaired down to hear his teachings in Tavatimsa heaven. The third heaven is Yama heaven, a heaven of bliss, also called the heaven of no attack. The fourth heaven is Tushita heaven, another very popular vacation spot. This is the heaven with the greatest sensuous pleasures — sex, food, music. This is where Prince Siddhartha lived as a deva prior to his birth because this is the traditional residing place of the Buddha-to-be.

Today, the future Buddha of Compassion, Maiteyya is currently a deva residing in Tushita heaven. He is awaiting the proper causes and conditions on Earth, to take rebirth (usually in India). Buddha prophecized that Maiteyya would become the fifth Buddha in this kalpa (age). Buddhism must first be wiped out from the world in order for the next Buddha to arise. This will happen. That is how kalpas have always gone. We don't know when this will happen. It depends upon our karma, how we nurture the dhamma. This may take many thousands or hundreds of thousands of years. The Buddha was Buddha number four in this particular kalpa, which is a big string of Buddha's to have in one kalpa! Aren't we lucky. Tushita heaven is more formless, or less structured than Tavatimsa. Tavatimsa heaven is a heaven of order. Heaven's first law is order; earth's first law is order as well.

In the fifth heaven, the devas delight in the power of creation. In the sixth heaven the devas delight in the power over the creations of others. That means that the devas of the top heaven in the sensuous sphere have power over the devas of the lower heavens, as well as the rest of the sensuous sphere, which includes all five of the lower realms. Mara lives on the outskirts of the sixth heaven. Mara is the ultimate embodiment of ego and a symbol of Mara is Darth Vader from *Star Wars*. Darth Vader had a highly attained mind and his powers of concentration were mighty. Mara is the Buddhist equivalent of the Christian devil, Satan. The Bible says that Satan was one of seven angels but he was bad and challenged God so he got cast down into hell and rules over hell. The Buddha teaches that Mara lives in the comfort and indulgence of heaven but has administrative powers over hell and all the rest, except for that which is above the sensuous sphere. The maras are a whole category of devas which are trouble makers, similar to the asuras except they're not all bad. Mara is not trying to pull you down to hell. He is the tempter who tried to thwart the Buddha's enlightenment. He will used food, money, sex, power to snare you. He just wants you working for his program. The good news is that the maras cannot penetrate up to the fine material sphere. All those brahmas are virtuous and they are so high they are not called devas.

'Seventh heaven' is a quantum leap up from the sixth heaven. The way to get there is through meditation by entering into jhana. When this happens you slip off Mara's radar screen and he can't find you. So if you are in a meditation absorption then you are above Mara and he can't affect you. Now we are into the big time — the Brahmaloka. These are the greatest, vastest, god-like devas in the entire cosmos. This is where Brahma lives for a life span of one whole cosmic cycle — 40 billion years by one translation of the abhidharma. He is the first deva born into this universe from the world of radiance, after the big bang. Brahma believes that he is God because he is there alone for so long that he has forgotten his birth and assumes that he created the universe. After a few eons passed he wished for company and he believed that he created the other devas that later appeared (by the process of their own karma). Those devas also believe that Brahma must be God and they all share this mistaken assumption that Brahma is the one and only absolute creator God, until some Buddha came along and tapped Brahma on the proverbial shoulder and told him that he is not an absolute almighty God; he's just one brahma. Brahma has an ego.

Brahma is limited by the self, self consciousness. An enlightened person, the Buddha, is higher than 'God' Brahma. Brahma is the Hindu God and he lives within the first three of the four layers of this fine material sphere.

Not all of the devas are Buddhists. Many devas have a theistic relationship with Brahma, believing that he is God almighty. Sakka told the Buddha about a time when Brahma paid them a visit at his celestial palace. He was sitting around the big table with the gods of the three and thirty when suddenly a beam of light came down. They immediately knew what it was so they perked right up and said "Brahma's coming! That's the signal!" Out of the beam of light appeared a gandharba, the lowest level of the devas. The Buddha described 28 classes of celestial beings. Brahma is such a high god that he can't even relate directly to the devas of the lower sensuous sphere, let alone human beings. So Brahma created an intermediary and he sent this gandharba described as Five Crest. Each of the devas of the thirty three believed that Five Crest walked up to only them, but this was an illusion created by the vast mind of the God-like Brahma. This is what Sakka described on one of his many visits with the Buddha.

Other non-Buddhist devas include Christians. There could be one group of Buddhist devas sitting around chanting the suttas and nearby another group of devas who are Christians praising God and Jesus. Because of their virtue as good caring Christians, they took rebirth in heaven as devas, believing that what they heard on Sunday was true because now they are in heaven. The belief system can carry over. Devas don't necessarily know about Buddhism.

In the lower realms, the ghost realm is inhabited by real ghosts, just like what you see in the movies. As described in the last chapter, it is commonplace to take rebirth there and there are happy and unhappy ghosts. They were probably people who have died and they are hanging around for months or years. The ghost realm is highly populated so you can assume there are ghosts on the streets, in public and private places. They generally can't harm you; they are a lower realm and we should have compassion for them; you can send loving kindness to them. The tradition from the Buddha is to use and chant the Ratana sutta to take care of problems with ghosts. Sometimes they can affect your mood, or the family in the house. What you do is you download and chant the two page sutta out loud in English, which is fine, and you sprinkle drops of water from a bowl with your finger tips, around the whole house, while you are chanting. This is what the Buddha did with Ananda and a prince in an area with many ghosts.

Ghosts have been known in every culture throughout every period of human history but science just dismisses this without comment, or simply with denial. Science generally doesn't relate to the evidence for ghosts. You can go on-line and see photos of ghosts and read more evidence. A huge percentage of people believe in ghosts because many have seen spirits themselves or have friends that have. I have heard stories from the people in my classes and certainly believe them. I lived in our Ajahn Chah monasteries in England in 2004 and I stayed at Chithurst monastery and discovered that it's commonly known there that a ghost inhabits one particular room of the men's dorm and it may have been there for a hundred years as it is an old mansion. It was purchased at a low price because people knew it was haunted. In a talk Ajahn Sumedho described that ghost as a malevolent spirit. I decided to stay in that room, even though other people had freaked out and left but I sat inside and did loving kindness meditation for the ghost, sending good vibes to it, repeating "May you be well, happy and peaceful." This was a preemptive 'metta' strike. I don't know if it worked but I didn't have any problem.

Since our loved ones who have died will likely spend some time in the ghost realm it is recommended that you do a practice for them which you can read in more detail on my theravada.ca website, called "The Significance of the Transference of Merits to the Departed". By dedicating merit to them you can give them a real boost in the ghost (peta) realm. When I lived at Amaravati Monastery in England a nun shared her impression with me that there are more ghosts in England than in Thailand because the Buddhists in Thailand are dedicating merit to their relatives and friends who have died and that helps the ghosts to move on and take rebirth as a human.

The hell realm is rock bottom in samsara. Hell is not at all a popular subject in the West, however it is not logical to believe that hell does not exist simply because it is unpopular. The Buddha described hot hells and cold hells, hells of moans, hells of screams and hells of indescribable filth. In Buddha's description of one hell, he said that it was like a man going into a shop which provides wheat. There are eighty bushels of wheat and once every one hundred years he takes one grain of wheat and walks away. Then a hundred years later he comes back and takes one more grain of wheat, and walks away. The amount of time it would take him to empty all of the bushels of wheat is the length of time that beings stay in this particular region of hell. Then Buddha went on to explain another part of hell where beings stay ten times longer than that! So Buddhism is not some new age teaching that we're all moving up to love and light. There really is a hell, sorry. Buddhism actually props up some crucial Christian religious beliefs. Christian purgatory could be called the hungry ghost realm and I'm convinced that the Catholics got it directly from the Buddhist ghost realm teachings.

Meditation Practice and Cosmology

During the final phase of my month retreat in Thailand, which was a necessary initiation before ordaining as a monk, we were instructed to make a great effort to attain a jhana. My meditation instructor, Phra Sawat said that I reached what is called the 'arising and ceasing of phenomena,' where you feel pin prick sensations all over your body. At first I thought there was an ant crawling on my knee, but then I realized that this was what I was waiting for. This is a stage prior to what is called 'neighbourhood concentration,' which occurs before a jhana, the jhana being a state where all five senses are absent.

This information is included in this chapter on cosmology to relate the deva world to our meditation practice. There are eight layers of the Brahma realms corresponding to the eight jhanas in total. Your meditation experience relates to the most far out mystical regions of Buddhist cosmology. It is not as though the higher regions of heaven have nothing to do with you. Some rare people can get into these jhanas, because they are putting time and effort into their practice and they may have less karmic obstructions.

The formless sphere is the top four layers of samsara. Here, these mental beings have no form at all, no kandha of body. This is kind of a spiritual dead end street because they need to come down to a lower level, like human, to get enlightened. These are: the sphere of infinite space, the sphere of infinite consciousness, the sphere of nothingness, and the top layer of heaven, the top layer of samsara, the sphere of neither perception nor non perception. This is not as good as being in the fine material sphere.

The Buddha's discourses are full of hundreds of stories of devas coming down and helping people or sitting beside the Buddha, patiently beckoning him to teach them. Devis are female devas. Devis are typically described as being exquisitely beautiful, topless and breathtaking in appearance. Just heart stopping beauty! Paintings or statues of devis in Buddhist temples often depict them as having pointed crowns on their heads with crests on either side of their head and crests pointing up on their shoulders. They are covered with gold, diamonds and jewels and beautiful flowing things. The beings of the sensuous sphere, which includes the five lower realms are driven by the urge towards sexual union. The brahmas of the two higher spheres are beyond sexual identity; they are asexual beings. An important point about the sensuous pleasure is that the disadvantage of going to heaven after you die is that you might not get much meditation practice in, or studying done to further your spiritual path if you're indulging in pleasures all the time. The god realm is like an expense account. After you've expended your honestly earned merit, then you fall from that birth like a lavish company account that is cut off when you are suddenly fired from your job. In the *Numbered Discourses Book of the Threes* the Buddha actually taught that most devas go down to the lower three realms after they die. Deva death happens when their luster fades. They are then shunned by other devas. Following this they have a horrific vision of where they will take rebirth, and then they die and go down to the lower realms.

In your previous lives you likely have already been devas as well as beings in all of the realms, human, ghost, animal and hell. You have traversed the galaxy because samsara is so long — billions of lives. The Buddha actually made it a precept for his monks and nuns not to join him just to reach a deva rebirth, that would be an offense. Your goal is higher than that, the Buddha admonished. Your goal is to go beyond the bliss of the god realm and attain full and complete enlightenment. For a monk to be reborn as a deva by accident is like a booby prize!

The good fortune of the human realm is that we have the advantage of suffering. Because we suffer, we are motivated to do something about our suffering. We get Buddhist books or we take a course to find someone who can teach us how to practice and meditate. It's usually some form of pain that brings people onto the path, so thank your stress. As Jesus pitied the rich young man because he couldn't leave behind what he had, to discover something better, you can appreciate the rightness and the goodness of being disillusioned with the sensuous pleasures in the world so you can care more for the spiritual path and devote more time to that.

Enlightenment takes you off of the wheel of life, finally, to the extinction of rebirth. Nirvana is beyond our ability to even describe accurately. Like a fish trying to understand a turtle's description of dry land, we cannot know what the experience of enlightenment is until we're there.

I had an interview with Ajahn Sona and asked his advice concerning my meditation practice, during which I visualize the devas in

Tavatimsa heaven. This meditation practice is called the recollection of deities. He told me:

In visualizing heaven, instead of mysterious things like lights and so forth which don't necessarily tell you a lot, you want to move toward images of a true sense of real happiness… the sanest I have ever felt… a true sense of joy and contentment… the clearest and the most joyful, and so forth. These are the images you want to conjure.

The devas enjoy sanity, that's the primary characteristic of heaven. Their definition of heaven is that it is very orderly. Sanity is order; beauty is order. What is sanity other than beauty? That's the word 'happiness' as in the British definition 'a happy painting', in other words, is when it has beautiful proportions to it. Happiness is when everything is in aesthetic proportion.

All religions have heavenly mansions. There are two levels of goals. The common level is aspiring to the heavenly mansions. That's perfectly fine. Its part of the Buddha's teaching and will strongly appeal to people. Nibbana will not appeal to many people. It's too abstract, it's too difficult to understand. But heaven? Well, fine! Remind people it's not the final goal. They may not be able to relate to the final goal right now. Keep it at the back of your mind on the way.Why is it a mansion? The human realm is symbolized often as a forest but the heaven realm is symbolized as a mansion because a mansion is artificial, it is constructed. Whereas the human realm is natural. The lower realms are chaotic so chaos and violence are the criteria. Nirvana is stillness itself. The heavens are defined by beauty and order and this is a created order. In a sense when we create the earthly mansions we are trying to imitate the heavenly mansions. The artist, the architect, when they have these images that they are attracted to, they're memories. They're utilizing memories from previous heavenly experiences and that's why people marvel at these things. It's beyond the human realm, it's divinely constructed. The heavenly realm is a combination of the exact symmetry of the mind and is spontaneous. The realm and the mind are not two things; they're the same thing. Often it's described that one wishes and there it is! So some people carry a lot of virtue on earth. They wish and it appears very rapidly, whatever they wish, they go very, very clearly towards that. In regards to meditation practice you can't expect people to never have a problem. Problems are manifestations of the mind. What protects you is virtue. Just get back to your

A Short Walk On An Ancient Path

virtue. Clear up your life, become virtuous and you'll feel at ease around anybody. You won't feel less than anybody. A peasant can be with a king and feel OK, because of virtue. Basic sanity lies in virtuous behaviour, the capacity to know what virtuous behaviour is. That leads to a sense of orderliness, a sense of happiness like an aesthetic order in the mind. And then the mind will be more in tune with heaven. As in heaven so on earth; as on earth so in heaven. This is the message of many religions. Christ talked about this. There is often confusion about this, but this is what is meant. Order your mind. Create a heavenly consciousness within your mind. Heaven is within or heaven is amongst you. Amongst who? Those who act in a divine way.

Ajahn Sona's advice encouraged me to reduce my emphasis on visualizing the details of heavenly mansions and to focus more on the uplifting feelings associated with the meditation. The recollection of deities practice is one of the 38 objects of meditation taught by the Buddha. Here, 'deities' means 'devas'. Buddhaghosa commented on this deva meditation practice in his fifth century *Path of Purification,* which says that by using such practices you become dearly loved by the devas. The idea is to contemplate upon the devas' qualities of generosity, virtue, faith, learning and wisdom. Humans took rebirth as devas because of these qualities and when you contemplate that you have these qualities within yourself, you are cultivating them. As monks in Thailand we did the recollection of the deities practice in the main Viharn. We also practiced the recollection of the Buddha and the recollection of the sangha. We would visualize the Buddha in the sky above and in front of us. This represents something that is higher and beyond ourselves. We would visualize Sariputra and other senior disciples arranged in the sky around the Buddha, at the same time chanting a beautifully melodic Pali chant.

Buddhist cosmology explains the ground under one's feet and the Hubble space telescope's discoveries. Any astronomer who has not studied the Buddha's teachings on the physical universe doesn't have adequate knowledge about the history of the science of astronomy. In Carl Sagan's popular 'Cosmos' television program in 1980 he had an episode describing how science and religion are far apart on their views. Then, he added a little footnote saying to the viewing audience that eastern religions are closer to science's view of astronomy. Then he just left the audience hanging by not admitting what the Buddha taught. Much of their viewing audience was in the American Bible belt so I can understand that the network did not want to upset people over the subject. Compare Buddhist cosmology to the book of Genesis in the Bible that has a cosmology that dates back to the fourth millennium BC. I couldn't live with that. I don't know who can.

The Buddha's description of the physical universe comprises some of the most astounding teachings he ever gave. I can still remember the chair I was sitting on in 1994 in Thailand when I read that the Buddha was the progenitor of something like the big bang theory. Actually, the Hindus may make the same claim as they teach this as well. History is uncertain about what happened first in India, because Indian history is notorious for not being too concerned about history. During my innocent boyhood years in the 1970s my father told me about this new theory called the big bang theory. He said that astronomers say that the universe blew out from a single point smaller than my thumb. It blew out and will likely collapse in again, maybe in 40 billion years or it may dissipate into entropy. The Buddha described periods of expansion and periods of contraction but it may not be as small as your thumb. Science is always revising theories so the Buddha's theory may be more accurate than our current astronomy. The Buddha taught that over vast periods of cosmic time 'Island Universes' form. I was amazed to learn this because those are galaxies. Someone could have guessed the existence of stars and planets in the 5th century BC but there is no way with the naked eye they could have guessed the existence of galaxies. Galaxies weren't discovered until the 1920's, by Astronomer Edwin Hubble. It was the Buddha's direct realization which allowed him to see galaxies in ancient times. Being enlightened, he could see the big bang or the beginning of the expansion. Buddha described solar systems as world systems and planets as world spheres.

No Spiritual Seniority System

One of my first Buddhist teachers almost twenty years ago explained to a group of us that if someone has been practicing meditation for twenty years and studying the teachings of the Buddhadharma for twenty years, then it is possible that they may not be as spiritually advanced as a new young person that just walked in the door the day before. This is because the new person who just learned how to meditate for the first time and who just started learning about the dharma yesterday, may have already reached great levels of meditative attainments in previous lives. Some people are just naturally more concentrated and together than others, regardless of their age, education or background.

So, there is no spiritual seniority system in the Buddhist religion. That may be part of the reason why the Buddha rebuked Ananda, his faithful attendant, when Ananda suggested that the Buddha should name a successor to lead the sangha after the Buddha's death. The Buddha knew full well that such a thing would create more problems than it would solve. The Buddha deliberately wanted the Buddhist religion to be decentralized and not controlled by any hands of power; he didn't want something like the Papal lineage to happen to Buddhism.

There should be a political seniority system within the sangha, for people to relate to each other and to relate to the conventional world. And, there is; much respect is given to a monks' seniority but Buddhism undercuts the idea of a bona fide spiritual seniority system between human beings. The Buddha did classify people into the four levels of sainthood, but it is not easy for the unenlightened to make such distinctions in others. The four levels of sainthood are: stream enterer, once returner, non returner and an arahant.

A stream enterer is someone who will reach enlightenment within seven lifetimes. They have attained to the level of a fundamental shift in thinking, as though they had seen only one side of the

Buddha's hand all of their life, then suddenly they see the other side. A once returner will only return to human birth one more time. A non returner will never take rebirth again as a human being, but is not yet enlightened. By process of elimination, they will be reborn as a brahma and attain enlightenment as a brahma. Lower down in heaven, even the devas can get enlightened though many people think they are indulging in too much sensual pleasure and bliss. Many devas genuinely do have that problem, but some areas of heaven are better than others for attaining enlightenment. Heaven is not all the same. Devas can become fully enlightened and continue with their very long life spans before leaving us for nirvana or wherever enlightened ones go. The Buddha left that as a mystery. An arahant has finished his work, he's fully enlightened, like a man who's been blind all of his life, suddenly being given sight.

You cannot measure or easily discern a person's spiritual attainments. In the Mangala sutta below, the Buddha counted the 38 highest blessings in life, and the third highest is to pay respects to those worthy of honour. It is easy to pay respects to well known people. It is not so easy to pay respects to those unsung heroes who have done much to create enlightened society. If you find them and pay respects to them, then you are fortunate. This sutta is a popular chant for asking for blessings and prosperity. You could focus your mind on what you are asking for and then chant it 1, 3 or 9 times. It's also a practical list of what actions matter in life.

Mangala sutta Chant for Blessings and Prosperity

Men, together with deities, tried to find out for twelve years what blessings were. But they could not find out the blessings which number thirty-eight, that are the cause of happiness.

Oh, Good People! Let us recite those blessings which were taught by the Deity of the Deities (the Buddha) for the benefit of beings and which destroy all evil.

Thus have I heard. At one time the Blessed One was dwelling at the monastery of Anathapindika in Jeta's Grove near the city of Savatthi. Then a certain deity in the late hours of the night with surpassing splendor, having illuminated the entire Jeta's Grove, came to the Blessed One. Drawing near, the deity respectfully paid homage to the Blessed One, and stood at a suitable place; standing there, the deity addressed the Blessed One in verse:

Many deities and men, desiring what is good, have pondered upon just what blessings were. Pray tell me what the highest blessing is.

Not to associate with fools, to associate with the wise and to honour those who are worthy of honour. This is the highest blessing.

To live in a suitable place, to have done meritorious deeds in the past, and to keep one's mind and body in a proper way. This is the highest blessing.

To have much learning, to be skilled in crafts, to be well-trained in moral conduct and to have speech that is well spoken. This is the highest blessing.

Caring for one's mother and father, supporting one's spouse and children and having work that causes no confusion. This is the highest blessing.

Giving, practice of what is good, support of one's relatives and blameless actions. This is the highest blessing.

Abstention from evil in mind, abstention from evil in body and speech, abstention from intoxicants and non-negligence in meritorious acts. This is the highest blessing.

Respectfulness, humbleness, contentment, gratitude and listening to the Dhamma on suitable occasions. This is the highest blessing.

Patience, obedience, meeting those who have calmed the mental defilements and discussing the Dhamma on suitable occasions. This is the highest blessing.

Practice that consumes evil states, a noble life, seeing the Noble Truths and realization of Nirvana. This is the highest blessing.

The mind of a person (an Arahant) who is confronted with worldly conditions does not flutter, is sorrowless, stainless and secure. This is the highest blessing.

Having fulfilled such things as these, beings are invincible everywhere and gain happiness everywhere. That is the highest blessing for them."

A naga guarding the entrance to a Thai temple

A Short Walk On An Ancient Path

Chapter 6

Why Buddhists Meditate

Rule number one is silence
Remember the golden rule

Three meditation yogis were on a silent meditation retreat for years deep in the forest, living in a cabin. They were sitting on the porch having tea one day, when a black horse came running by. They maintained their silence for a year and then the first yogi said "Did you see that brown horse run by?" They fell silent for another year, then the second yogi said "That wasn't a brown horse! It was a black horse." Another year of silence went by and then the third yogi finally said "If you two don't stop this incessant bickering, I'm going to leave!"

Like Siddhartha Gotama, if you today attained enlightenment and broke through the delusion of your society and you became the greatest spiritual being of your age, you would expect to live a public life that would become progressively more and more quiet as you pulsated wisdom and love through the sleepiness of the infrastructure around you. Visualize yourself as a completely enlightened person. You move more slowly and peacefully and the world bends space around your anatta (non self) waves. Silence is golden. Your inner work is done. You love all beings and your only purpose now is to teach others. Each decade you are alone because the leader is always alone. You recline in a TV studio and communicate with the world. Your presence inspires others to build a greater vision and they respect your enlightenment by speaking only the words that are needed. No matter how many people are moved and stirred by your inspiration, you yourself live a quiet little life. Now you sway in the rocking chair of your quiet little life, holding your seat as a living arahant. It is a useful affirmation to visualize how this enlightenment could manifest itself in the 21st century. Until then you can study the dharma, practice meditation, talk about Buddhism, help others, and continue to develop.

When I was living in Bangkok, Thailand I was teaching courses on Buddhism and meditation to other foreigners in Bangkok. I was often confronted with questions about Thai cultural affectations which people assumed to be representative of Buddhism. In beginning a talk on Buddhism I often didn't know where to begin to describe what it was all about. Before my short time in the monkhood I lived in Chiangmai where I started a meditation and discussion group. At one gathering we didn't have any particular plan so Robert began the discussion by saying that earlier in the week he was stunned to see a man smash a dog across the back with a stick. Robert asked the man why he was doing this and the man explained that in a previous life the dog had been a bad army general so it deserved this beating. I cringed inside and muttered feebly that I didn't think that this was a very good way to start off our Wednesday night get-together. If anyone is so highly attained that they can see into the previous lives of a dog, then they would not be the type of person to break a dog's back with a stick.

So, what is a good way to start a discussion about why Buddhists meditate? The teachings are so vast, the realization of the Buddha was so sublime and the dhamma has such a path quality. There is a huge treasury of psychological teachings in Buddhism, which is less developed in other religions. In my classes I sometimes say that Buddhism is similar to psychotherapy, but it is more than that. Buddhists should make commitments to working with their minds and hearts. The Buddha taught ways of dealing with our thought patterns to overcome our neuroses. That may help people feel more comfortable if they don't like the word 'religion.'

Buddhism has three stages: virtue, mental purification, and insight or wisdom. Virtue, or morality discipline means intending to live within the precepts that the Buddha prescribed. The general concept of proper moral conduct is similarly shared with other religions and humanistic philosophies. Where Buddhism really takes off is in the stages of mental purification or serenity and insight. Sitting meditation and walking meditation plus post meditation practices of mindfulness in daily life, build up concentration. It is this concentration that naturally leads to the fruit of insight. As my first teacher, Chögyam Trungpa Rinpoche said "Buddhism has more to do with the kitchen sink than with the high and holy."

Building concentration is like raising the water level in a great dam. As you meditate the water is going up and up until it reaches the top of the dam. Then, that water is used for energy to create power — electricity. That is insight. Without the foundation of morality, it is as though holes have been smashed through the walls of the dam. No matter how much you meditate, it won't add up to one drop if you are seriously violating precepts against such things as killing, stealing or fooling around. If the integrity of your character or the wall of the dam is secure, then when the water of concentration reaches the top in the practice of meditation, this naturally leads to insight. Insight, or wisdom is produced in meditation practice by formalizing and systematizing this natural process which we call meditation, or bhavana-mental culture, cultivating the mind. When you stare at a sunset, and dwell upon the orange sky and the beautiful clouds, that is a form of meditation. Concentrating on making money is a form of meditation which can also aid you in attaining insight. Insight is not something that you can collect or cash in after a half-hour of sitting on the cushion. You cannot open your eyes and say "I want my insight now. I've worked for it. I've paid for it." Insight comes when it is ready to come. It could take years. Insight could manifest as a sudden, important realization, or a deeper understanding of yourself, your strengths and weaknesses. Insight also means seeing into the true nature of reality, the three marks of existence: suffering, impermanence and non-self. The ultimate insight engulfed the Buddha under the bodhi tree when he attained full and complete enlightenment. You should know when genuine insight wells up within you. It is not the usual assortment of pleasant or discursive thoughts that you sometimes have. It is clear and bright, complete and meaningful to you. Sometimes meditators have false insight. I had that in 1993 after a one month retreat in Thailand when I believed for a day that I was enlightened. Then reality caught up with me and convinced me that I was not. That was embarrassing.

In the West the meaning of Buddhism is becoming closely associated with meditation and meditation retreats. I agree that meditation is essential on the path to enlightenment but right effort, and right mindfulness and right absorption, are just three parts of Buddha's eightfold path. The other five are right view, right intention, right speech, right discipline and right livelihood. The first, right view, means developing and understanding a precise view of the four noble truths, the eightfold path, the nature of mind, etc., but the Buddha also stated, "Right view is karma and rebirth", so karma and rebirth is very much the world view of Buddhism. A chapter of this book is devoted to that. Having a precise view is important, otherwise there is a danger that the practice of meditation could become self oriented. You could build up your concentration by meditating upon wrong views that take you off the path and reinforce the ego.

When you meditate you may think that you have a particular reason for practising meditation. You may be doing it to reduce stress, it's good for your heart or your blood pressure or meditation will help calm you down and make you a nicer person. All of that is true but they are only by-products of meditation. The Buddhist reason for why you meditate is to understand and follow Buddhist principles. That's a big, vast and ambitious reason for why you meditate. Meditation takes you deeper into the eightfold path and along that path to end suffering, gain the highest bliss, to transcend the limitations of the self and to shed off the tyranny of ego.

Bhikkhu Bodhi talks about why Buddhists meditate in his interview with *Insight Journal*, v. 19, 2002, titled "Climbing to the Top of the Mountain:"

The big question we face is whether and to what extent Buddhism should be refashioned to conform to the particular exigencies imposed by American culture. Throughout history Buddhism has generally adjusted its forms to enable it to adapt to the indigenous cultures and thought — worlds in which it has taken root. Yet beneath these modifications, which allowed it to thrive in different cultural contexts, it has usually remained faithful to its essential insights. This may be the biggest challenge facing Buddhism in America, where the intellectual milieu is so different from anything Buddhism has ever previously encountered that in our haste to effect the necessary adaptations we may be unwittingly diluting or even expurgating principles fundamental to the Dhamma. I believe we need to be very cautious if we are to find a successful middle way between too rigid adherence to traditional Asiatic forms and excessive accommodation to contemporary Western — and specifically American — intellectual, social, and cultural pressures.

It might be counterproductive to attempt to import into America a version of Theravada Buddhism that retains all the customs and mores of Southeast Asia. But I believe it is essential to preserve those principles that lie at the very heart of the Dhamma, and to clearly articulate the proper purpose for which the practice of the Dhamma is undertaken. If we tamper with these, we risk losing the essence along with the extrinsic accretions. In our current situation, I think the main danger is not inflexible adherence to established Buddhist forms, but excessive accommodation to the pressures of the American mind-set. In many of the Buddhist publications I have seen, I have detected signs of a widespread program, regarded almost as obligatory, to extract Buddhist practices from their grounding in Buddhist faith and doctrine and transplant them into a basically secular agenda whose parameters are defined by Western humanism, particularly humanistic and transpersonal psychology.

Can you point to ways this might be happening?

I think we see examples of this in the use of vipassana meditation as an adjunct or companion to Western psychotherapy. Actually, I'm not overly worried about psychologists using Buddhist techniques to promote psychological healing. If Buddhist meditation can help people feel more comfortable about themselves, or to live with greater awareness and equanimity, this is good. If psychotherapists can use Buddhist meditation as a tool of inner healing, I would say more power to them. After all, "the Tathagata does not have the closed fist of a teacher," and we should let others take from the Dhamma what they can effectively use for beneficial ends.

What I am concerned about is the trend, common among present-day Buddhist teachers, of recasting the core principles of the Buddha's teachings into largely psychological terms and then saying, "This is Dhamma." When this is done we may never get to see that the real purpose of the teaching, in its own framework, is not to induce "healing" or "wholeness" or "self-acceptance," but to propel the mind in the direction of deliverance — and to do so by attenuating, and finally extricating, all those mental factors responsible for our bondage and suffering. We should remember that the Buddha did not teach the Dhamma as an "art of living" — though it includes that — but above all as a path to deliverance, a path to final liberation and enlightenment. And what the Buddha means by enlightenment is not a celebration of the limitations of the human condition, not a passive submission to our frailties, but an overcoming of those limitations by making a radical, revolutionary breakthrough to an altogether different dimension of being.

This is what I find most gripping about the Dhamma: its culmination in a transcendent dimension in which we overcome all the flaws and vulnerabilities of the human condition, including our bondage to death itself. The aim of the Buddhist path is not living and dying with mindfulness (though these are, of course, worthy achievements), but transcending life and death entirely to arrive at the Deathless, at the Immeasurable, at Nirvana. This is the goal the Buddha sought for himself during his own quest for enlightenment, and it is this attainment that his enlightenment made available to the world. This is the end at which the proper practice of Dhamma points, the end for which the practice is undertaken in its original framework.

This end, however, is lost to view when insight meditation is taught as just a way to live mindfully, to wash dishes and change baby's diapers with awareness and tranquility. When the transcendent dimension of the Dhamma, its very raison d'etre, is expunged, what we are left with is, in my view, an eviscerated, enfeebled version of the teaching that can no longer function as a vehicle to deliverance. Though correctly practiced, the Dhamma does bring abundant happiness within the world, ultimately the teaching is not about living happily in the world but about reaching "the end of the world" — an end that is to be found not in the far regions of outer space but within this fathom-long body with its senses and consciousness.

So you do not think Dhamma is being taught as a path of deliverance?

The impression I get from what I've read in contemporary American Buddhist publications is that this aspect of Buddhist practice is receiving little emphasis. I hear of students being taught to accept themselves; to live in the present from moment to moment without attachment and clinging; to enjoy, honor and celebrate their vulnerability. Again, I don't want to underestimate the importance of approaching the practice with a healthy psychological attitude. For a person troubled by self-condemnation, who is always dejected and miserable, the practice of intensive meditation is more likely to be harmful than beneficial. The same might be said of a person who lacks a strong center of psychological integration or of one who tries to deny his weaknesses and vulnerabilities by presenting a façade of strength and self-confidence.

But I have to emphasize that the training that accords with the Buddha's own clear intentions presupposes that we are prepared to adopt a critical stance towards the ordinary functioning of our mind. This involves seeing our vulnerabilities, i.e., our mental defilements, not as something to be celebrated but as a liability, as a symptom of our "fallen" condition. It also presupposes that we are determined to transform ourselves, both in the immediate moment-to-moment functioning of our minds and in their more stable and persistent extension over time.

To take up the Buddha's training is thus to draw a distinction, even a sharp distinction, between our characters (proclivities, dispositions, habits, etc.) as they are now, and the ideals to which we should aspire and seek to embody by our practice of the Buddhist path. The mental dispositions we must acknowledge and seek to rectify are our kilesas, the defilements or afflictions: the three root-defilements of greed, aversion and delusion, and their many offshoots such as anger, obstinacy, arrogance, vanity, jealousy, selfishness, hypocrisy, etc.

So the great affirmation to which the Buddhist path points us is not the wonders of our "ordinary mind," but of the mind that has been illuminated by true wisdom, the mind that has been purified of all taints and corruptions, the mind that has been liberated from all bonds and fetters and has become suffused with a universal love and compassion that spring from the depth and clarity of understanding. The practice of the Buddhist path is the systematic way to close the gap between our ordinary unenlightened mind and the enlightened, liberated state towards which we aspire, a state which rises to and merges with the Deathless.

To reach this transcendent goal requires training, a precise, detailed and systematic process of training, and fundamental to this whole course of training is the endeavor to master and control one's own mind. One begins with the development of such fundamental qualities as faith, devotion, moral virtue and generosity, proceeds through the development of concentration, and then arrives at direct insight and true wisdom.

Enlightenment remains enlightenment, beyond the space-time conceptual limitations of time itself, so there is then no longer any possibility of ever slipping back into samsaric ego mind again. This eternity is beyond time because it has got nothing to do with time. Enlightenment forever leaves behind the sleep of ego. Shortly after his enlightenment, someone asked the Buddha "Who are you?" The Buddha answered "I am awake." The Buddha taught that fully understanding the nature of enlightenment with words and concepts is impossible because enlightenment is well beyond conceptual mind. Like the words and concepts above, the Buddha too used many words and many concepts to describe enlightenment anyway because as he said, "The finger points at the moon." It does help to try to get some

A Short Walk On An Ancient Path

appreciation for what nibbana is like. You don't have to be a Buddhist to attain complete enlightenment. The Buddha wasn't a Buddhist. But the higher up the mountain top people get, in any spiritual path, the more they say and do the same things. The closer different paths get to the mountain top the more similar they are.

To attain enlightenment you don't have to go out anywhere to find it. Don't go to Tibet. It would help to take the time and effort to uncover your layers of ignorance, passion and aggression. Listen to that still small voice within. Why waste time through more hollow barren loneliness, birth, old age, sickness and death? Meditate and get moving on your spiritual path. To purify the mind you can pay the price of right effort now, or you can pay later.

Do you get up in the morning and plunge into your loneliness and depression? Trungpa said that taking the refuge vow begins an odyssey in loneliness. What do you think he meant? In those grey, sad minutes, you can visualize Buddhas sitting all along the horizon, 15 degrees high into the sky. See them as white and translucent with rainbow colours oscillating on the surface. Practice meditation or contemplation to go into your broken heart and out the other side. Cheer up! Enlightenment, the final breaking apart of your ego, is not some nihilistic wiping out of yourself that turns you into a big nothing. It is bliss and it is real. Imagine being able to penetrate to the truth about anything and revealing that to others.

Buddha images in a Thai Wat

Chapter 7

Non Self

"What lies before us and what lies behind us are small matters compared to what lies within us."
Ralph Waldo Emerson

In *Ulysses* James Joyce writes (Joyce, 1922; 572):

> Did Stephen participate in his dejection? He affirmed his significance as a conscious rational animal proceeding syllogistically from the known to the unknown and a conscious rational reagent between a micro and a macrocosm ineluctably constructed upon the incertitude of the void.

How close did James Joyce get to the Buddhist view which holds that there is no self? Buddhism rejects the self because of the certitude of the void. The void is not a big nothing. The void is the luminous and blissful. The certitude is that if you syllogistically and experientially unravel ego, from the micro to the macrocosm, such as Brahma, you will ineluctably fall into the ego's groundless feeling when the mind experiences glimpses of the void, egolessness. This unknown is beyond ego's territory — which is limited to the known. The reagent is that by going within your own microcosm in meditation practice, you can experience the macrocosm of the universe and step through the uncertainty of the void into nirvana. Good! Step into that groundless unknown. That's the route to go. So, the answer to James Joyce's 1922 riddle is that Stephen did indeed participate in his own dejection.

People often ask, how can there be rebirth if there is no self? If there's no self, what is it that takes rebirth? Unique to Buddhism is the view that your self is composed of five things, one part body (rupa) and four parts mind (nama). These five are collections, or aggregates of tendencies and characteristics called khandhas. Khandha translates from Pali to mean heap; group; aggregate; grasping, physical and mental components of the personality and of sensory experience in general. The second khandha grows out of the first and so on. There's no accurate English word to replace khandha, so let's use the word 'aggregate'.

These are the five aggregates of the self:
1.   Form or body
2.   Feeling — the five senses
3.   Perception
4.   Mental formations or thoughts
5.   Consciousness

You are not a thing, you are a process. You don't have a permanent identity. You are not a rock in the river, you are the river itself. And just as you can stick your fingers in the river to change the eddies and currents that flow downstream, just so you can change your life and your identity by altering your habits, your ethics and your mind. To understand the five parts, use the example of listening to a Buddhist teacher give a talk. You have your form, your body with the physical organ of the ear. You hear the talk because sound waves travel from the teacher's mouth and hit your ear. That's form, the first aggregate. The second aggregate of feeling comes into play when the sound registers in your ear and is transmitted to your mind. Then you perceive that there is sound and you recognize that the sound is a person talking and you understand what the words mean. That's perception, the third aggregate. You can see at this point that the process is getting more psychologically sophisticated with each step.

Once you understand the words that the teacher is saying you develop ideas about them. You may think that he makes sense, that he's profound or you may have questions in your mind; you may disagree with what's being said. This is the fourth aggregate of mental formations, your myriads of thoughts continuously going through your mind. Number four is a big one. We live our lives in our mental formations, don't we? This also includes your intentions and volitional actions, so this is where karma comes from, this is where you initiate your karma. Your awareness of your thoughts and the rest is consciousness, the fifth aggregate. This is the fruition of ego's complex game of building itself up. Consciousness in the case of unenlightened people, such as ourselves, is limited to self consciousness.

The big news that the Buddha laid on us is that this self does not exist as a permanent identity. You don't have a self in the sense that 'self' means something stable, permanent. *You do exist.* In the "Khandavaga" in the *Connected Discourses of the Buddha* by Bhikkhu Bodhi, the Buddha states that your body does exist, but it is impermanent, suffering and non self. He says that your feelings, perceptions, mental formations and consciousness do exist but they are impermanent, suffering and non self. It's important to point this out because some Buddhists go too far and they say that you don't even exist. You're just an illusion, a foam on the wave, but this is not true. You *do* exist and more importantly your suffering does exist, so you must do something about that. Shortly after the Buddha's great awakening he said to himself that what he had realized went against the grain. People do not want to know, people do not want to hear that there is no God, and that they do not have a self.

It is good to emphasize the five parts of non self that make you what you are. What you do have is quite a lot. All of your life, memories, hopes and dreams, and future incarnations are all wrapped up in form, feeling, perception, mental formations and consciousness. Everything in the idea of 'soul' is included here, except for permanence — that is permanent identity. The Buddha didn't use the words "There is no self", but the reason the Buddha taught anatta, non self, is because each of these five aggregates is impermanent. None of them can be called self. Even if you put them together and combine the five into one psychosomatic organism, there is still no real self there. The idea of self or soul usually implies an everlasting being of some kind. None of the aggregates is like that. Your physical life is impermanent, so your body is not your self. Your senses, perceptions and thoughts are fleeting from moment to moment. They are not permanent. They are not your self. Your consciousness, your self consciousness fades in and out like a TV set on the blink. Your consciousness of ego, of self, is also impermanent except that part which transcends the ego. When you attain to enlightenment you discard self consciousness and merge with the permanent state of enlightened mind. So, even though your ego is impermanent, the idea is that your goal is to shed off this impermanent ego which limits your mind to the idea of self and self limitation. But there is no ethereal link beyond the five khandhas holding them together in a transcendental way. There's just the five aggregates, rolling on.

Your consciousness and karma go with you from life to life but it is the idea that you have a permanent identity that is false, the Buddha teaches. Consciousness does not have an identity! When it rains, nobody is in the cloud making it rain. It's just natural processes playing themselves out. Just so, in the mind there is just thinking, memory and feelings. If you are Jane Smith in this life, there will not be an everlasting Jane Smith living happily ever after in heaven after you die. Your self concept of Jane Smith is a false assumption, so to speak, and after death your five aggregates will come together again in another form, perhaps as Sharon Jones in Vancouver. There will be no more you, no more Jane Smith. Jane Smith will be a buried past life memory in the mind of Sharon Jones. That's the idea of non self. You still continue, but you do not continue as the identity that you are now.

Closer to our own experience, you are still the same person today as you were when you were a baby, but in many ways you are not the same person now as you were then. Extending this process, when you are old and die, if you eventually take rebirth as a human baby, you will not be the same person as a baby that you were as an old person in your previous life. However, in another way, you will still be the same person as the baby that you were in the former life. You can see then that the five aggregates are rolling on and changing in every year, in every moment. There is no self in there that has any nucleus of identity. You are not the same person now as you were when you picked up this book, even moments ago. You've changed!

Buddhists don't like to use the word soul because it implies the false view of eternalism. But you could say that you do have an everlasting changing consciousness in the sense that your consciousness will never die. It continues on and eventually merges with nibbana if you attain enlightenment. However, there's no guarantee of that ever happening. So, the view is quite optimistic actually, because you live forever and then what happens after attaining nibbana is an uplifting mystery. There's no problem with not existing as a self.

The Buddha demonstrated a way of regarding the five parts of the self by comparing them to meat from a cow. The Buddha said that a butcher chops up a cow and sells sections of meat at a crossroads. He presents various steaks, hind roast, ribs, lean meat, etc. When people come to buy meat they do not ask for 'cow.' They do not say "May I have some cow please?" That would be silly. The butcher does not say "Yes. This is cow. You may purchase some cow from me." So, the self is gone. The self of the cow is gone. You regard the parts of the cow the way you should properly regard each of your five aggregates. In meditation or post meditation it is a good practice for you to mentally review your body, senses, perceptions, thoughts, and awareness, rather than thinking about 'you' so much. When you bite into a Burger King Whopper with Cheese, there is no need for you to have one thought about a cow, in order for you to contemplate the beef. That is properly considering the aggregate of form, body, without dwelling upon the ego identity of the cow. It's fine to thank the cow and to dedicate your merit to it to help the cow attain a higher rebirth, but that's another fine topic of dharma.

The actual experience of anatta, non self is an ordinary thing. If you get so absorbed in your household chores that you become one with what you are doing, that is an experience of egolessness. When I was living at Wat Pah Nanachat in Thailand, Ajhan Sumedo said that in meditation practice, you label 'thinking' when there is an itch on your right knee. There is only the feeling and the knowing mind, the 2nd and the 5th aggregate. There is no you there, there is no self there, he said. You don't think "I have an itch on my knee." There is just the physical sensation that is apprehended by the knowing mind. That's it and that's all.

Meditation practice is built upon the truth on anatta. Simple though the technique is, it is designed to poke holes in the walls of the ego, by cutting through the mental formations that constantly arise to shore up ego's defences. It is like the colours on the film of the soap bubble desperately trying to make sure that the bubble doesn't burst! When you label 'thinking' and come back to the breath, you are taking a miners pick and you are chipping away at the walls of ego. The practice is designed to bring you to egolessness by dropping your struggle and just letting be. The thoughts are always spewing out to convince you that you are the person named on your ID, but the Buddhist lineage has so skillfully constructed the meditation discipline that you always have a chance of breaking through neurosis and glimpsing the direct experience of non self.

There is ultimate reality and there is conventional reality. The Buddha used the conventions of speech that we always use when we say words like me, I, us, we, them, they, she, he, etc. There's nothing wrong with using conventions of speech when discussing conventional reality.

Just know that in ultimate reality there is no such thing as self, I, me, you, etc. The Buddha said "Monks, you must use conventional speech, otherwise you will not be understood."

Comparing the Hindu belief in the atman — the soul which reincarnates — to the Buddhist anatta, the Hindus have a simile in the *Bhagavad Gita* of a man who puts on a suit of clothes, then takes them off and puts on another suit. This represents reincarnation where the man is the same and his soul is the same, going from life to life with the same essence. Just his body differs from life to life. In Buddhism we have rebirth, not reincarnation, which the Buddha described with the Pali word poonapuva, which means 'again existence'. So it's not the transmigration of a self identical soul. It's the repeated occurrence of the process of becoming; a 'repeated becoming'. There is a continuity, a transmission of influence, a causal link up, but no soul, no permanent entity. We have a continuous flow of mental acts, thought moments, called "cittas". The citta arises and gains an impression from our senses and thoughts then it disintegrates and the next citta arises and inherits the impressions of the last one and so on. This is how our continuum of mind maintains our identity and we remain approximately the same human being throughout our lifetime even though no ego entity, no self, underlies this process.

What happens at the moment of death is that the last citta which arises is the death consciousness citta. This conditions the next citta which determines the whole realm into which we will be reborn and it will have a new physical organism as its basis. Buddhists believe that it is very important to die in a peaceful, wholesome state of mind because that can determine your whole next rebirth. Buddhists help the dying by reminding them about what a good person they were and how much they helped others, because they want to put them in a happy frame of mind. After a person takes rebirth, the cittas continue on in the next life. At death the self undergoes radical change with the loss of the body and the family and surroundings. As stated in the last chapter, most people probably take rebirth as a ghost. If they later return to the human realm they experience what the Buddha called "relinking consciousness" where conception occurs when the spirit, the gandharba, enters into a womb when there is the sperm and the egg making a suitable fetus. The simile is of a candle burning down, then you light a second candle as the first one goes out. The second candle is the same flame but it's burning on a different wick with different wax so it's a different flame as well. That's a simile for non self from life to life. Part is the same, but time moves on and change naturally happens. Another simile is of a bird which leaves its nest and builds another nest. The nest represents the body and bird is the mind. Building the nest is the time in the womb leading to rebirth.

Once a person dies and goes to the ghost realm they still crave sense contact so they need the sense faculties and organs. The entire organism is required, nama rupa, mind and body, because a being can't be suspended in space. When people die they lose the suitable basis for experiencing the pleasures of the world. They want the world of the senses so craving grasps for a new body and a new being gets conceived. That is why the Buddha called craving the seamstress. Ajahn Brahm says "We don't have the five senses to protect the body. We have the body to protect the five senses. The Buddha said the five senses are the world."

Ajahn Sona said (Sona, 2001):

> The Buddha's teaching was not mere reason or mere goodness or mere beauty. The Buddha was interested in a particular truth, the truth of the way to the end of suffering. Science is good at answering questions but wisdom knows the right question to ask. Intellect takes over the house and drives out the master of wisdom. The polar opposite of suffering is absolute peace. Like an arrow being pulled back the Buddha pointed out all the ways that you suffer. Firing the arrow goes to the bullseye of nirvana. We don't even see some of our suffering as suffering. Fish do not understand that they are swimming in water. Like sand in a jewel, it is the very grit that causes us to create the beautiful, the pearl.

The mind is a universal process. It's not personal. Your mind is not really your mind. You didn't make it. You don't know where it came from. How did you make it? Certainly your mind is unique but it's not personal. If you arrange the proper conditions and causes to produce the result of goodness, truth, beauty, happiness and enlightenment, then they will occur. If you don't arrange the necessary conditions and causes, then enlightenment cannot occur. You don't have to get rid of the clouds and then make the sky blue. The sky is intrinsically blue — clear blue. If you remove the hindrances then you can't help but feel peace, bliss, ease.

Grand Palace, Bangkok, Thailand

Non Self

Emerald Buddha, Temple area, Bangkok, Thailand

Chapter 8

Opening the Heart

"Use your heart to listen to the Teachings, not your ears."
Ajahn Chah

Delusion or ignorance can be compared to the idea of original sin in the Bible. In the book of Genesis Adam and Eve are in the Garden of Eden with God and they are not even aware of any difference between God, man, or woman. Then they do something terribly shameful by eating from the fruit of the Tree of Knowledge given to them by the snake. This was their original sin, because of which they were driven out of the Garden of Eden, and into exile. In Catholicism the idea of original sin is that deep down inside of you, there is something fundamentally wrong with you. Deep, deep down, you have a basic problem. That problem is original sin, so you have to be healed. You need to be saved. Your soul must be redeemed by the messiah, you need to be saved by Jesus, God. That salvation is like being granted reentry into the Garden of Eden.

In Buddhism, deep, deep down, your root problem is avijja, delusion. That's your most fundamental issue. Your problems arise from ignorance. But even deeper down than that, underneath your ignorance and delusion, some people believe that you have the seed of enlightened mind. This concept suggests that all sentient beings, limitless as space, have this great characteristic. You already have enlightenment within you right now, except that it is buried under your layers of confusion, they say. There is a sutta in the Numbered Sayings where the Buddha said "Monks the mind is luminous but it is defiled by adventitious defilements." Adventitious means not inherent; accidentally acquired; extrinsic. This one obscure statement by the Buddha was taken by some people who concluded that you have the nature of a Buddha deep within you. That's quite a leap; that's quite a jump to come to that conclusion. If that was what the Buddha meant he would have said it 1001 times. It occurs but once! Your mind is not luminous and defiled at the same time. It may be a skillful means to say that you have an enlightened mind within you right now: that you are a perfect Buddha, but that's not a great help. It's like saying to a sick person "Underneath your sickness you're very healthy actually." — "Well, that's good to know. That's a nice idea but I need relief." If you have a dirty table and you want to eat off it, it doesn't help to say that underneath all this dirt the table is intrinsically clean. That's true but it doesn't help the situation. The point is that you have to clean off that table first. This buddha-nature or bodhicitta teaching is a Mahayana concept but Mahayana Buddhism first arose about 500 years after the Buddha, around 50 BC. So, the Buddha never taught the Mahayana.

The Buddha said he came for the benefit of the many, he didn't say that he came for the salvation of all. Buddhism denies predetermination. Without "X" there is no "Y." If you don't apply effort to create the conditions for enlightenment, it won't happen. There is no ontological reason to say that all beings will get enlightened. If that were true then there would be no need for effort! One student in my class even threatened to leave the course unless all beings were going to obtain enlightenment.

Connecting with your heart and cracking through your numbness is analogous to connecting with your parents. Suppose you take a trip to Mexico with your beloved parents. You are all on the beach having a good time. You get tempted by some rather attractive looking locals

A Short Walk On An Ancient Path

and you wander off with them and get carried away. It's the height of tourist season and the beach is a completely mad festival of multitudes of happy people (the scriptures define a multitude as being 84,000 people). When you come back you cannot find your parents. You search the beach, scanning up and down, but they are nowhere to be found. You've lost your parents. The analogy is that you were once connected to your heart but because of your neurotic thinking you're now out of touch.

Twenty years go by, and you haven't seen your parents; you think about them now and again. You go on vacation to Long Beach on the west coast of Vancouver Island, Canada, with your own young family. As the humongous cold waves shimmer across the sun baked sand, you feel a rare and sacred peace after working so hard all year long. An elderly couple are seated nearby, but you don't pay them no never minds, until you sense something familiar. You hear a familiar voice so you look again and you see your parents sitting right there. You go over and introduce yourself and they feel as awkward as you do. You all agree to have lunch over at the Beach House and it is there that you notice the many idiosyncrasies that remind you of your youth spent with them. Only then, after being with them for some time do you breakdown and cry because you know that you have finally been reunited with your parents, like the Adventures of Odysseus. That's connecting with your heart, awakened heart. The Buddha said, "It doesn't matter how long you forget, only how soon you remember."

The Buddhist concept of ignorance is not the same as original sin in Catholicism. Using the comparison of the Garden of Eden, there is a Buddhist image of the Buddha sitting under the tree of immortal life, sitting in the ultimate peace of nirvana. Nearby, protecting the Buddha is a naga. When you walk into a Buddhist temple the nagas are protector devas depicted as statues of serpents placed so that you would have to get by them first in order to see the Buddha. This is very similar to the scene at the gate of the Garden of Eden. There you have a tough looking figure, a cherub, standing at the gate and God is saying that the guard is emphatically there and that you can't get in! But as you peer in to see the Buddha, the Buddha is holding up his hand and he's saying to you "Don't worry about those nagas at the gate, they're not going to hurt you. You can come in." So, you step inside and you sit under the tree of immortal life and you find your transcendence to nibbana. Buddhism leads you to the still point within, to the end of your spiritual journey, but the Bible is basically a religion of exile.

The moment of exile from the Garden of Eden can also be compared to the five hindrances. This is the delusion and confusion of mind which constantly prevents us from getting to the peace and stillness which can be found within us, like getting back to the Garden of Eden. That inward journey to attain enlightenment means to go into your heart. Ralph Waldo Emerson said "What lies behind us and what lies before us are tiny matters compared to what lies within us."

So, how do we connect with our heart? How do we realize awakened heart? We must be willing to face our state of mind. In the sitting practice of meditation, we sit and we look at our minds, ourselves, our inner being, our true nature. In meditation we confront our state of mind, we work with our mind as it is. You are searching for your heart, your naked beating heart. Beginning with meditation practice there are many techniques which guide you to opening your heart and making your heart more available to others. Meditation is the way to touch and let go, touch and let go. By looking into your mind, you look into your heart. In this way you can share your heart with others. Because there is so much suffering in the world it is not best to be self stuck in the bliss of the god realm state of mind but as you grow in happiness you naturally enjoy sharing that with others. George Bernard Shaw said "Enjoying happiness without producing happiness is like spending money without earning it."

If you could touch your heart, if you could put your hand in your chest and touch your heart, you would feel tenderness. Even if a feather lands on your heart, you feel so touched. Your heart is open to the world. You don't have to go on a rampage of hugs and kisses and throw flowers in the air as you dance and sing in the street, to extend warmth towards others. If someone speaks to you in the supermarket line up, you may feel bothered but you can listen to them and warm up to them. To chat with them is compassion in that moment, in that situation. Each hour presents different moments of kindness, different opportunities to uplift others. Having compassion for all sentient beings means that 'sentient' is 'of limited awareness,' so the Buddha was not a sentient being because he did not have limited awareness.

The dharma path is described as a process of working on yourself before you have the skillfulness to go outwards and work with others effectively. If a person doesn't work on himself first, he/she could be like the well meaning person that sees someone lying in the street after a car accident. They pick the victim up, accidentally severing their spine, then put them down at the side of the road. When working with others, one must avoid the missionary mentality of laying a trip on people and shoving 'the truth' down their throats.

Loving Kindness, Compassion, Joy, Equanimity

Opening your heart to others is easier to do if you have training. A treasury of psychology teachings is provided to invoke more heart and loving kindness for others and for yourself. The Buddha taught a series of four contemplations called the divine abodes — loving kindness, compassion, joy, and equanimity which crack open the numbness around your heart. Appreciate that 'your' heart is very similar to someone else's heart, so how can you watch them suffer? How can you not want them to be happy?

There is some sense of stages to these four contemplations. The Buddha called these the brahma viharas. Here we draw from Buddhaghosa's famous commentary *The Path of Purification,* written in 412 AD in Ceylon. Buddhaghosa writes that the word divine means that you put your mind at the level of the most divine devas, who are brahmas, who live in the fine material sphere, or brahma world, of the god realm. These practices can put you there in your state of mind. Abidings means that you live or associate with these vast God-like brahmas, as though you are one of them.

The general purpose of these four contemplations is the bliss of insight and obtaining a beautiful and excellent form of future existence, meaning your next rebirth. Considering all the time and money spent by people to look beautiful, they should invest in their future beauty by doing these contemplations. For those who have the foresight to take good care of their skin while they are young, they already have a disposition to take the long time perspective, which is wise, so it is not radical thinking to be planning ahead for one's good looks in the next life.

Peculiar to each of the four respectively is the warding off of ill will, cruelty, aversion (boredom) and envy, and greed or resentment. As to the characteristics of each, loving kindness is characterized here as promoting the aspect of welfare. Its function is to prefer welfare. It is manifested as the removal of annoyance. Its proximate cause is seeing lovableness in beings. It succeeds when it makes ill will subside, and loving kindness fails when it produces selfish affection.

Compassion is characterized as promoting the aspect of allaying suffering. Its function resides in not bearing others' suffering. It is manifested as non-cruelty. Its proximate cause is to see helplessness in those overwhelmed by suffering. It succeeds when it makes cruelty subside, and it fails when it produces sorrow.

Joy, or gladness is also called altruistic joy because it is characterized as gladdening produced by others' success. Its function resides in undercutting envy or jealousy. It is manifested as the elimination of aversion (boredom), its proximate cause is seeing the success of others. It succeeds when it makes aversion (boredom) subside, and it fails when it produces merriment.

Equanimity is characterized as promoting the aspect of neutrality toward beings. Its function is to see the equality in beings. It is manifested as the quieting of resentment and approval. It's proximate cause is seeing ownership of deeds (karma) thus: 'Beings are owners of their deeds. Theirs is the choice by which they will become happy, or will get free from suffering, or will not fall away from the success they have reached'. Equanimity succeeds when it makes resentment and approval subside, and it fails when it produces the equanimity of unknowing, which is that [worldly-minded indifference of ignorance] based on the householder life.

There's a story from Buddhaghosa, though it's not in the suttas, that the Buddha taught this metta practice to a group of monks. The monks were being tormented by devas who were trying to drive them out of their home region because they had overstayed their welcome. The devas created fearful appearances and foul smelling odors. The monks got up, all at once, and left and went to the Buddha to ask for a better retreat location. The Buddha said, "No. You must go back to that place." "But what about those fearful apparitions and the foul odors?!" the monks protested. "Before you were without weapons", the Buddha taught. "Now, I will give you the weapons of loving kindness." So he taught them the metta practice and they went back and their retreat was very successful; the devas loved the monks, and in return they made their rains retreat very pleasant by making food appear and by conducting them to their kutis to meditate.

The technique for the loving kindness contemplation is described in chapter two. The other three contemplations are done in similar ways. Loving kindness means an attitude of friendliness towards all beings, gladness, happiness. It is like the Greek concept of agape which made an impression upon the philosophy of Martin Luther King Jr. Dr. King said that when he was in university he struggled with the problem of how to love the white southerners who were oppressing the blacks. King actually studied Buddhism in university but it was Greek philosophy that made more of an impression on him. He said that he was moved by the idea of a disinterested love for all mankind, which is found in agape. He discovered that he didn't have to be best buddies with the racists, he did not have to associate closely with them, he only had to love them from afar. This is the Buddha's teaching on metta.

Buddhaghosa extensively described the benefits of doing the loving kindness contemplation. He describes the results of loving kindness practice as being that you sleep in comfort and fall asleep as though entering upon an attainment, you wake in comfort like a lotus opening, you dream no evil dreams, devas guard you, fire, poisons and weapons do not affect you, your mind is easily concentrated, the expression on your face is serene, you die unconfused, after death you will reappear as a brahma in the fine material sphere as one who wakes up from sleep, you are dear to human beings and you are dear to non human beings.

Buddhaghosa tells the story of an Indian man, the Elder Visakha who heard that the island of Ceylon was 'apparently adorned with a diadem of shrines and gleams with the yellow cloth, and the environment is favourable.' He made over his fortune to his wife and children and set off for Ceylon where he ordained. In *Path of Purification* Buddhaghosa writes (Nanamoli, 1956; 338):

When he had acquired five years' seniority and had become familiar with the two Codes, he celebrated the Pavarana at the end of the Rains, took a meditation subject that suited him and set out to wander, living for four months in each monastery and doing the duties on a basis of equality with the residents.

On his way to Cittalapabbata he came to a road fork and stood wondering which turn to make. Then a deity living in a rock held out a hand pointing out the road to him.

He came to Cittalapabbata Monastery. After he had stayed there for four months he lay down thinking 'In the morning I depart.' Then a deity living in a manila tree at the end of the walk sat down on a step of the stair and burst into tears. The elder asked "Who is that?" — "It is I, Maniliya, venerable sir." — "What are you weeping for?" — "Because you are going away." "What good does my living here do you?" — 'Venerable sir, as long as you live here non-human beings treat each other kindly. Now when you are gone, they will start quarrels and loose talk." The Elder said "If my living here makes you live at peace, that is good," and so he stayed there another four months. Then he again thought of leaving, but the deva wept as before. And so the Elder lived on there, and it was there that he attained nirvana.

This is how a person who abides in loving kindness is dear to non-human beings.

Compassion contemplations sometimes begin with contemplating one's mother. The idea is that the mother image kick starts a feeling of love and compassion because we are supposed to have the most love for our mother. You contemplate thus: "My mother has taken care of me from the moment I was conceived in her womb. She suffered hardships giving birth to me, nursing me, cleaning away my filth. She taught me to do good and she steered me away from evil. Because of her incredible kindness I have now met with the teachings of the Buddha and am practicing the dharma, while she herself still wanders in samsara! How sad I feel in my love for her. The least I can do is help clear away her suffering." You arouse genuine compassion in this way and extend it to your mother, and you continue from there and send compassionate thoughts to all other beings.

Loving kindness is love directed to all beings. Compassion is love directed to those who are suffering. Altruistic joy is love directed to those who are happy. The give and take contemplation on compassion is a Theravada answer to the Tibetan Mahayana Buddhist practice called tonglen. In tonglen you breathe in black and breathe out white. In this Theravada practice you breathe in white and breathe out white. The Tibetans do the 'black in' to take on the suffering of others, then 'white out' to give them compassion. I have found that when I'm sick I like to be around people who are healthy. It's not going to help the sick if you get down beside them on their sick bed and try to make them feel better by getting sick yourself! From a Theravada view, it's not necessary to take on the suffering of others. You can just send them compassion for their suffering. This practice is not as important as loving kindness because the Buddha taught that metta should be made a habit of, frequently practiced, developed, made much of', "one should sustain this recollection". The Buddha also taught different ways of meditating on compassion — similar to the metta technique. The Buddha didn't teach this give and take technique but it is here because it's a correction for the tonglen practice and it's another way to express compassion.

Contemplation on Compassion

The technique is that you sit in meditation posture, close your eyes and think of someone whom you want to extend compassion to, someone that you easily feel compassion for. You could start with your mother. You imagine that you are breathing in white luminosity from space. It doesn't really matter where it comes from. This is bright compassion and you're breathing it into your whole body, filling your whole body like a container, not just your lungs. You do this practice on the medium of the breath at the nostrils so you have your mouth closed.

On the out breath you visualize that moonbeams of white light are streaming out from your nostrils into the other person, displacing their blackness, displacing their suffering. Imagine that this light encapsulates all of your love, virtue, happiness, health, wealth and goodness from your past, present and future — anything good that you've got! — you're giving it away to others. Then you breathe in the limitless luminosity of compassion again, filling your body up like a vessel. Keep repeating this with natural breaths. Avoid the temptation to suck in long breaths. You can just take one salami slice of compassion at a time.

You can spend a few breaths on one person, then move on to your family and friends and so forth. Send it to everyone in the room, groups of people and beings, to war torn countries, everybody in the world, etc. You can follow the same sequence as in metta. You can even breathe the luminous love into negative encounters you have had with people. This practice is primarily done for the suffering and pain of others but you can use the 'white in, white out' practice to heal your own physical, mental or emotional suffering. If you have a sore back as you sit in meditation, you can breathe out the healing white light to yourself. Do the same to take the tension out of anticipated future events, like job interviews. If you had a miserable childhood or a deep depression in your life, you can even go back in time and breathe love and compassion into that chapter of your life and rewrite the history books. Why not?

Because you are so focused on light and love, at the end of the give and take you should dissolve the visualization and go back to your breath meditation practice for a couple of minutes before you stop otherwise you might get a headache.

In the post meditation environment you can use the white in, white out as well. If you are driving in your car, you can breathe it out to people on the street. Even if someone is talking to you, in the midst of a conversation you can breathe in the light and extend this compassionate feeling to him or her. Like exercising a muscle, you can develop this practice as a lifestyle of compassion so that you automatically switch into it. Don't worry if you're not good at visualizing. It doesn't matter. It's just the thought that counts — the feeling. Just the idea of sending compassion to beings is all you need. "All you need is love."

I taught give and take to a class in a Vancouver temple and later one of my students practiced it for a friend of hers who was having an operation. As Lindy held her friend's hand during the operation, she practiced give and take without telling the other woman what she was doing. Later her friend said "I feel great! I feel like all this blackness and yuckiness and tar has been sucked right out of me!" That was astonishing for Lindy but it is not uncommon. Another woman taught it to her five year old son while he was in the back of their car, asking what they could do for the many suffering street people. She explained it to him while she was driving and the little boy loved the practice and he did a good job of it. You can teach this to children.

This practice inclines you towards compassion, it trains you to develop a habit, an attitude of compassion. Usually you feel better after the practice, like you can actually do something for others. Often you can't do much for those who are suffering even though you want to.

To do the contemplation on altruistic joy, like the compassion practice above, you can use my guided meditation CD. You think of someone you know who is really happy. If you don't know anyone, you can think of someone that you don't know personally, or you can imagine someone. You could visualize happy families skiing in the Alps. They're rich and full of good character and charm. Everybody likes them. You feel their success and you tune into that. You get vicarious joy from imagining their joy.

Equanimity is a highly attained state of mind which is not flustered by the vicissitudes or joys of life. No matter what activities you are engaged in, you have an evenness of view. You may be the CEO of a Fortune 500 company. One minute you are putting a stamp on an envelope, then another minute you are making decisions affecting the jobs of a thousand employees. It's all the same to you as you flow in the space of undisturbed equalness.

An example of equanimous behaviour occurred when President Kennedy went to parties during the Cuban Missile crisis. Before the President went public with the crisis, the Soviets assumed that he didn't know what was unfolding. Kennedy knew what terrible possibilities of nuclear war were at stake but he remained in the present moment. Secretary of State Dean Rusk had what Bobby Kennedy described as "a complete physical and mental breakdown," during the crisis. President Kennedy had secret audio tapes of the cabinet meetings made, which have been published. His generals were advising him to just fly in and blow up the missile silos with everyone there, but Kennedy, not wanting to kill hundreds of Russian engineers and technicians, took the middle way and ordered a blockade of the island instead, resulting in no loss of life. Even without his Secretary of State to help, Kennedy maintained equanimity masterfully. Equanimity is like an eye in the sky stretching from horizon to horizon.

The Buddha said "If you knew what I know you would say "A-ha! Marvellous." Happiness is number one on the list. Buddha said "Find the beautiful; swim in the beautiful." How do you arrive at beauty and truth except by beauty and truth? Strive for the good, the true and the beautiful. This has been a description of the four contemplations to awaken the heart. If you practice them and develop these states of mind, you will swim in the beautiful.

Grand Palace, Bangkok

Monks in a Thai temple

Chapter 9

The Five Hindrances

*"Science is good at answering questions
but wisdom knows the right question to ask."*
Ajahn Sona

The five hindrances are everything that stand between you and a completely clear, happy and enlightened mind. This is one of the most practical Buddhist teachings because it teaches you the antidotes to get rid of the five hindrances which are: sensual desire, anger, dullness and drowsiness, restlessness and worry, and doubt. Another way of putting it is: moving toward, pushing away, sinking down, rising up, flurry and worry and spinning around. The Buddha took the mass of confusion in our minds and he divided it into these five neat categories with specific antidotes for each one. The list is always in the same order for ease of memorization. This gives us confidence that we can get a handle on our minds and work with them successfully. You're not properly practicing mindfulness meditation until you take care of these hindrances. The five hindrances are the cause of delusion. What is the cause of the hindrances? The cause of the hindrances is unwise attention, unwise reflection. It is the absence of wise attention to an object. So you look at an object, unwisely attending to it and you see only a partial picture. What you see is the repulsive, the unbeautiful and if you see only that, ill-will, anger arises. For lust you attend unwisely. You see the beautiful. You do not see the whole picture, you zero in on the beautiful "I want." Therefore with desire, craving arises — the first hindrance of sensual desire.

You don't stand a chance against the hindrances without mindfulness. Mindfulness attracts virtue from memory; it pulls it out of memory. Memory is very selective. It likes similar conditions so if you're meditating, memories bubble up from the past. If you provide a space that is similar to virtuous behaviour then the words and images which will flow up will be skillful. They come back to you. You want to start pulling those up. Like attracts like so the skillful will come up. That's where forgetfulness comes from too. Forgetfulness is the opposite of mindfulness so when you're in a lusty state of mind you forget all your good advice. It's not there. It's not available because other advice that is connected with why you should act on all your desires comes up instead and fills your head with every Rolling Stones song that prompts you to act on every impulse!

The Buddha used a simile to describe sense desire, ill-will and delusion. He compared sense desire to a cloth with a small stain that is difficult to wash out. Anger is like a large stain that is easier to wash out and delusion is like a large stain that's also very hard to wash out. Sense desire is a small stain because it's not as damaging to society and anger. It's hard to wash out because sense desire is accompanied by pleasant feeling and society encourages sense desire. Our economy thrives on advertisements that entice you to buy silly things you don't need. Store front displays lure you in. Whereas anger is a large stain because it's much more damaging to society and your relationships than sensual desire and it's intrinsically uncomfortable. You never wish that you will get a good anger on today so you look for ways to avoid anger. That's why it's a stain that's easier to wash out. Delusion is difficult to wash out because we don't recognize it. Delusion presents itself as knowledge. People act on wrong information believing that they are right and then later they see their mistake, hopefully. The word 'avija' translates as delusion or ignorance but it just means a lack of knowledge. The word ignorance has an unsavoury element to it as if a person is defective or something so I think delusion is a better word to use.

Below are sections of a great little booklet called *The Five Mental Hindrances and Their Conquest* by Nyanaponika Thera. You can do a search and download it for free. For years I have carried it around in my bag for my talks. Nyanaponika and Nyanatiloka Theras were two German Jews who fled Hitler in the 1930's and made their way to Sri Lanka. They ordained as Theravada Buddhists monks and started the Western Buddhist monk tradition, you could say. They were great scholars and did much writing and translating in English and German and they founded the Buddhist Publication Society where Bhikkhu Bodhi trained with Nyanaponika. Ironically, during World War II the British threw them both into an intern camp together, from 1939 until a year after the war in 1946, because they were Germans!

Nyanaponika writes (Buddhist Publication Society, 1993; 1):

> Unshakable deliverance of the mind is the highest goal in the Buddha's doctrine. Here, deliverance means: the freeing of the mind from all limitations, fetters, and bonds that tie it to the Wheel of Suffering, to the Circle of Rebirth. It means: the cleansing of the mind of all defilements that mar its purity; the removing of all obstacles that bar its progress from the mundane (lokiya) to the supramundane consciousness (lokuttara-citta), that is, to Arahatship.

> Many are the obstacles which block the road to spiritual progress, but there are five in particular which, under the name of hindrances (nivarana), are often mentioned in the Buddhist scriptures:
> 1. Sensual desire (*kamacchanda*),
> 2. Ill-will (*byapada*),
> 3. Sloth and torpor (*thina-middha*),
> 4. Restlessness and remorse (*uddhacca-kukkucca*),
> 5. Skeptical doubt (*vicikiccha*).

They are called "hindrances" because they hinder and envelop the mind in many ways, obstructing its development (*bhavana*). According to the Buddhist teachings, spiritual development is twofold: through tranquility (*samatha-bhavana*) and through insight (*vipassana-bhavana*). Tranquility is gained by complete concentration of the mind during the meditative absorptions (*jhana*). For achieving these absorptions, the overcoming of the five hindrances, at least temporarily, is a preliminary condition. It is especially in the context of achieving the absorptions that the Buddha often mentions the five hindrances in his discourses.

1. Sensual Desire

The hindrance of sensual desire comes first because it's generally the strongest. You can ask yourself which hindrance is your strongest, and which is your second strongest. You have to be clear with yourself about what is wrong with sensual desire because we're enticed and pulled in many directions. Strong forms of sensual desire take the form of an obsession to have sexual intimacy, great food or fine music. Remember that sense pleasures are fleeting and true happiness cannot be found in the pleasures of the five senses. True happiness has to be found within with the cultivation of the heart, in meditation. People complain that the Buddha is saying that we can't have any fun but the truth is that really you don't. It's disappointing. The Buddha gave the simile that sense pleasures are like taking out a loan. After your pleasure is satisfied it must be repaid with the hollow emptiness of waiting for your next sensory hit and you have to work towards that, so it's like being in debt. If your pleasure is an expensive hobby then you have to pay a lot of money for it.

Six things are conducive to the abandonment of sensual desire (BPS, 1993; 9):
1. Learning how to meditate on impure objects;
2. Devoting oneself to the meditation on the impure;

A Short Walk On An Ancient Path

3. Guarding the sense doors;
4. Moderation in eating;
5. Noble friendship;
6. Suitable conversation.

That's a handy list above for the antidotes to sensual desire. Explaining them in more detail, meditating on impure objects is seeing the unattractive aspect of what you desire. When I ordained as a monk in Thailand, the first contemplation they gave me to focus on was "hair of the head, hair of the body, nails, teeth and skin." All of it is dead. The idea is to reduce sexual desire by concentrating upon the unattractive aspects of the body. The Buddha listed 31 parts. An extra one was added centuries later, the brain, because up until the second century AD the ancient world did not regard the brain to be much more than bone marrow, a coolant for the blood. So if you are trying to curb your attraction to the opposite sex, think of their large intestine and their small intestine, their bones, stomach, urine, etc. This contemplation is helpful for monastics because they have to be celibate. But even for lay people it's another technique in your collection in case you need it.

Guarding the sense doors means to look away when you see something that arouses lust. It's so simple but it's worth stating. Guard over the doors to all five senses; be mindful of what you see, hear, taste, touch and smell. I like going to the Birken Forest Monastery. It is a low sensory environment. It is quiet with a peaceful atmosphere; there's no TV, music or traffic. That's the idea of a Buddhist monastery so I take that as a reference point for my life. In my 20's I needed to listen to lots of pop music but today just a little bit now and then is fine. That's the middle way. I like to be in a quiet apartment because it's more natural for me now. Controlling, as well as you can, what comes into your five senses enables you to live a more contemplative life and go in a more meaningful inner direction. Desires are latent; see what causes them to arise. If you're shopping for shoes just get shoes. Don't come home with a coat and a TV. That just creates more desires. From boredom sensual desire can arise and the rest of the hindrances. With desire, if you fight it, it seems to excite the same energy so it's good to slow it down. If you hold just one still image of the object of your desire in your mind its energy is reduced.

Noble friendship and suitable conversation apply to the other hindrances as well. This means that when you feel you are weakening you call someone who has experience and is a good role model for you, who is more composed and dignified and mature and is not given to strong sense desire or another hindrance. Just by seeing them or talking to them they can uplift you and help you. This is similar to a twelve step group. Suitable conversation is to talk about ways to overcome the hindrances, talk conducive to detachment, to freedom from passion, tranquility, contentedness, higher knowledge, talk about virtue, concentration and wisdom. The Buddha said "The entire holy life, Ananda, is noble friendship, noble companionship, noble association. Of a monk, Ananda, who has a noble friend, a noble companion, a noble associate, it is to be expected that he will cultivate and practice the Noble Eightfold Path. – Samyutta Nikaya (SN) 45:2

For each of the five hindrances the Buddha gave a simile comparing it to a pot of water. Sense desire is like a pot of water filled with bright colours like red, yellow and orange so that you can't see your reflection in the water.

2. Ill-will

Five Ways of Removing Distracting Thoughts

The second hindrance is ill-will, anger, aversion. This can range from mild irritation at the weather to livid murderous rage. Even depression is a form of aversion because when you're depressed you're saying that you're not happy with reality as it is; you don't accept it, you are adverse. Fortunately, the cures for anger apply to depression as well. The Buddha compared ill-will to being sick. If a man has a bilious disease and he receives nice sweet food, he won't enjoy the taste because of the sickness and he will just vomit it, complaining that's its bitter. In the same way, an angry man will not enjoy much of anything and he will reject the advice or constructive criticism of others.

Anger is the acid test of any religion, isn't it? "How should people deal with anger?" is a question that is put to any humanistic philosophy or method of psychotherapy. The Buddha gave us five techniques in Middle Length Discourse No. 20. Read it online. The first is thought substitution; you replace an unskilful thought with a more skilful thought. If you're angry, switch to loving kindness. The simile is of a carpenter or a carpenter's apprentice knocking out a course peg of wood with a smooth fitting peg of wood, so you should constantly be shifting your thoughts from the negative to the positive. You shouldn't just sit there with your depressing moods. If you're resentful towards someone you have to interrupt the process, not just watch it, and then introduce goodwill and probably not directed to that person if it won't work. Send goodwill to an easier subject to displace the ill-will. It's like making espresso coffee. You infuse it with steam. Right effort means you infuse your mind with wholesome good thoughts. The more you know that, the more you can do it. The more you do it the better you will get at it. Some people just sit there in meditation and don't change. They need some espresso or 10W-40 oil, if I can mix my metaphors.

In the second method, the Buddha said that if you have an evil, unwholesome, unskilful thought you should regard the thought with revulsion and just reject the thought. Suppose it's a repeating thought pattern that you're fed up with, think of it as the corpse of a dead dog on a necklace around your neck. Just as you would feel revulsion and disgust and quickly remove the dead dog, just so, push that thought out of your mind. Some methods are stronger than others. If one technique doesn't work, then try the next one.

The third practice is to give lack of attention to the thought, just forget about it, and that's the basic breath meditation instruction isn't it? If you have a thought, what are you supposed to do? Just ignore it and come back to the breath. The simile the Buddha gave is of a man walking down one side of the road and he sees an acquaintance of his walking towards him on the other side of the road. Instead of crossing over and inquiring about his health and his family and so forth, he just lets the man pass by. Just stay on your side of the road and let them stay on their side of the road. If a thought comes in one side of your head, just let it pass out the other side. Just let it go.

The fourth method is stilling the thought formation, by gradually slowing down the thought and stopping it. The simile is of a man walking quickly down the street and then he thinks, "Why am I walking so fast? What if I were to just slow down?" Then he slows down and while he's walking slowly he thinks, "What if I were to just stand?" and he stops and stands. Then he thinks, "Why am I standing? What if I were to sit down?" and he sits down. Then he thinks, "Why am I sitting? What if I were to just lie down?' and then he lies down. I always make sure he lies down on the side of the road because I don't want him to get run over. You can see, what you are doing is you are taking the gas out of the thought pattern. You can't just stop this type of thought so you are gradually slowing it down; then you just knock it out. And if it comes back again just do the same practice again. I sometimes imagine putting a white plastic bag over the thought, on the right side near my head, then I gently squeeze the bag down to nothing, and I throw it in the garbage. If you are in supermarket with a two year old and he has a temper tantrum, you can't just tell him to stop that. You've got to get his attention and grab a banana and say, "Hey! You want a banana? Or do you want your soother?" Then you slip the soother into his mouth and distract him until he's a quiet gurgling toddler. Experiment with this technique and find your own way of visualizing your thought formations, and slowing them down.

In the fifth method in sutta 20, the Buddha recommended suppressing the unwholesome thoughts by pressing your tongue against the palate and clenching your jaws to crush mind with mind and beat down and subdue that evil, unwholesome, unskilful thought. He used the simile of a big strong man who grabs a weak puny man and holds his head underwater and drowns him. You hold that negative thought underwater and drown it, then let it float away. This is an intense technique and it shows how serious the Buddha is that you can't just sit there with your negative, depressing thoughts. You've got to do something about them even if you have to clench your jaw. Modern psychology doesn't like this method but you will not become a repressed individual doing this. Repression can happen unconsciously in a trauma but suppression is the wise decision to hold back your reaction now because it is inadvisable or dangerous to react with anger. Using these antidotes to bring a hindrance to cessation does not make you a suppressed, repressed individual.

The Buddha taught several other methods to deal with ill-will. He instructed that you can regard others with onlooking loving kindness, onlooking compassion or onlooking equanimity. You can also just avoid people that upset you. You don't have to remain in every difficult relationship and work it out. Sometimes it is better to leave, but you can't always do that if the difficult person is your boss. If someone is persecuting you, you can reflect on the law of karma. The Buddha said that you can contemplate that they are the owner of their actions, heir to their deeds, their deeds are the womb from which they are born, the kin for which they are responsible and all that they do, to that they will fall heir. So this gives you some solace knowing that what goes around comes around. The Buddha taught that you can contemplate in this way to reduce your aversion. You can also be philosophical about karma, thinking that the reason why this person is being so mean to you is that you may have been mean to them in the past and this is your own karma ripening. Or, you can think of them as a conduit through which your past negative karma is ripening so this could reduce blame. But you should still be proactive and do something about your predicament as you don't know your past karma.

The Buddha said "Being angry with another person, what can you do to him? Can you destroy his virtue and his other good qualities? Have you not come to your present state by your own actions, and will also go hence according to your own actions? Anger towards another is just as if someone wishing to hit another person takes hold of glowing coals, or a heated iron rod, or of excrement. And, in the same way, if the other person is angry with you, what can he do to you? Can he destroy your virtue and your other good qualities? He too has come to his present state by his own actions and will go hence according to his own actions. Like an unaccepted gift or like a handful of dirt thrown against the wind, his anger will fall back on his own head."

Letting emotions pass through you is another technique that applies to any emotion or disturbance. You can cultivate the energy of your negative emotions. The way in which emotions arise, dwell and pass away is that you deal directly with any negative emotions as they arise in your mind. This may be a bit more difficult to practice if you're in the middle of a fist fight with somebody, but even then this technique is applicable. What you do is that you "stare down" your anger, your passion, jealousy, envy, whatever it is. You bring your attention to it in your mind and you stare it down. This means that you do not act out your anger, you do not actually "get angry." You also bring your attention to the physical feelings associated with your anger but you do not follow the thoughts. Closely observe the knot in your solar plexus, your clenched jaw, the shoot of heat going up your spine and neck, etc. This is mindfulness/awareness.

The whole point is that you should observe your anger rather than engaging your anger with your body, speech and mind which generates negative karma for yourself. Instead of getting angry at others you should avoid spreading more anger in the world and deal with your own mind first. It will not help the world for you to express your anger. Break the anger response.

Ideally, if you can sit in meditation or control the environment around you, that would be good. If you are in your office and you slam down the phone in a huff, take that opportunity to quietly sit and meditate upon your sensations. This is your opportunity to turn almost certain bad karma around and make it a moment to bring your negative emotions onto your spiritual path. The energy of anger can be cultivated just as manure on a farmer's field is cultivated to bring fresh new crops into being. Bring your mind inside your body. As unwholesome thoughts tumble and rumble through your mind, boycott your thoughts but stay with the feeling. Feel your pain. Experience your experience. Don't get into the mental rationalizations about that no good so-and-so because that will only entrench anger deeper into your mind. Your objective is to get rid of your anger and you can do that by going right into your anger. You go through your anger and out the other side. Fearlessness doesn't mean being without fear, it means stepping into fear and going beyond fear.

You can study Chinese medicine and add the visualization method where you bring the energy up your spine to the top of your head and then down the front of your body to your naval. You put your tongue on the palate. This completes the circuit of the internal orbit of energy within the body. Chinese medicine and Chi Gong and yoga have much to offer when it comes to working with energy. When keeping vigil over your feelings, your emotions take on a translucent quality, they become flimsy and fall apart. Anger is not consistent, with no gap. The truth of dukkha is that all things are impermanent so in this technique, when you put your focus keenly on your feelings, they eventually shift and change and their energy is sort of transmuted. Boycott your thoughts — but stay with the feeling.

What happens is that anger is associated with the lower chackras, and you are bringing that energy up, out of the top, as it were. "Chackras" refer to channel wheels or energy centres in the body, but the Buddha never taught about chackras. This is a Hindu idea that arose after the

Buddha but some Buddhists dig the concept anyway. This is not to say that chackras don't really exist but we can conclude that it was something that the Buddha didn't feel was important for him to include in the dhamma. The idea of this practice is that as you bring your energy up, your experience of anger fades and you begin to feel alright. You want to keep on using your new found strength.

Transforming and upleveling your emotions is possible and this is an opportunity for you to practice the path of dhamma even in the worst situations of your life. So when you feel miserable... just cheer up! Keep in mind that there are other ways of dealing with anger but loving kindness is the main method that the Buddha taught. Metta dissolves your aversion at a deeper level. Letting emotions pass through you is a stop gap measure to deal with this hindrance in the heat of the moment. Anger will still come up again so you still need to apply the antidotes and have a regular metta meditation practice to keep up an effort to eradicate it.

These are all practices to work with the tempestuous angry mind. The Buddha compared a man who is freed of ill-will to a sick man who has been cured by his medicine. He regains his taste for honey and sugar just as a man realizes that ill-will causes much harm and learns these methods to let go of this hindrance. The simile for the hindrance of ill-will is that it is like a pot of boiling water. You can't see your reflection properly when you look into the pot.

3. Dullness and Drowsiness

The third hindrance was translated as 'sloth and torpor' because 19th century translators in England and Germany, who first brought the Buddha's teachings to the West, chose those words. Not the best choice. 'Dullness and drowsiness' is a more common term. Who uses the word torpor? This is the least of the hindrances in meditation and we get it often. Not having enough sleep is not a hindrance. Just go and sleep, fine. But the genuine hindrance has two parts which both have mental unwieldiness. One is dullness as in mental inertia and the other is drowsiness as in sleepiness. When this comes up in meditation don't just sit with it. Do something about it. The Buddha taught that you should make an effort to overcome sleepiness. Try to burn through it. Rouse your energy, stir up your energy. Meditation is the opposite of sleepiness, it's about wakefulness, mindfulness, awareness. The Buddha compared dullness and drowsiness to being in prison. You're cut off and you can't appreciate what is going on when you are dozing off. If a person slept one hour a day less, for 80 years and they were awake 16 hours a day or more, that would add one sixteenth to their life; that would be five more years added to their life! Wouldn't that be worth it? The Buddha gave various methods to overcome dullness and drowsiness. Here are techniques taught by the Buddha, including my commentary, followed by some other suggestions.

1. Open your eyes and look downcast a few feet in front of you. The light coming in will keep you awake because you can't sleep with your eyes open.
2. If that's not enough then raise your gaze and look all around and look into a light. The Buddha would tell monks meditating at night to look at the moon.
3. Splash cool water on your eyes and face. It keeps you awake as it evaporates off your face.
4. Pull and shake the ears and rub the limbs with the palm of your hands.
5. Walk with your senses turned inward, with your mind not going outwards, conscious of that which is before and behind.
6. Change posture and stand.
7. Knowing that overeating is a cause of it; eat four or five mouthfuls of food less than you usually do at a meal because it takes time to hit bottom before you know that you feel full. It's those last mouthfuls of food when you stuff yourself that cause the blood to have to come down to the stomach to digest the huge mass, which makes you sleepy.

8. Visualize light. The subconscious mind doesn't know the difference between a real experience and a vividly imagined one, so this can keep you awake.
9. Meditate in the open air. Get outside open to the sky.
10. Noble friendship. Talk about overcoming dullness with a good role model who is not given to dullness and drowsiness.
11. Suitable conversation. Talk with others about the disadvantages of sleepiness and sleeping in.
12. Contemplate upon your own death. Who knows when death will come so now is the time to exert yourself on your spiritual path and have a sense of urgency.
13. Perceiving the suffering in impermanence. The Buddha said "In a monk who is accustomed to see the suffering in impermanence and who is frequently engaged in this contemplation, there will be established in him such a keen sense of the danger of laziness, idleness, lassitude, indolence and thoughtlessness, as if he were threatened by a murderer with drawn sword." – AN 7:46
14. Meditate on sympathetic joy. It you tune into others' happiness it energizes you.
15. Contemplate the spiritual path. An indolent person can't follow the path of the attained ones.
16. Contemplate the greatness of the master, the Buddha. "Full application of energy was praised by my Master, and he is unsurpassed in his injunctions and a great help to us. He is honoured by practicing his Dhamma, not otherwise." -Vism. IV, 55
17. Contemplate the heritage of the great law. I have to take possession of the Good Dhamma but one who is lazy can't take possession of it.
18. Abandon whatever thought is making you sleepy.
19. Keep the mind stimulated by mentally reviewing the teachings.
20. Learn some Dhamma by heart and recite it to yourself from memory.
21. Adjust the meditation object. If the mind is drowsy, that's not the time to do meditation on tranquility, concentration and equanimity. It's time to meditate on energy, and rapture and reality.

You could repeat a mantra to get your energy up (obsessive worry can help too).

22. Finally, if you do have to sleep, lie down on your right side in the lion's posture, with the left leg on top of the right. You lie on the right side because the heart is on the left so there's less physical pressure on the heart. Determine what time you will wake up, thinking 'I won't indulge in the pleasure of sleep.' Get out of bed as soon as you wake up.

Some other techniques are:

23. See the knower and the doer. Calm the doer but enhance the knower, keeping it awake.
24. Take an active interest in the process of sleepiness. Be mindful of sleepiness, noting "Sleepy, sleepy, sleepy." Like the skipping of a stone across the water, the mind sinks down and then noting and taking an interest causes the mind to perk up again.
25. For really serious people, sit at the edge of a well or at the edge of a cliff! That'll keep you awake.
26. Lie down with your head on a coconut, or sit on an uncomfortable surface. Charles Lindbergh took the cushion off his seat when he flew across the Atlantic. He stayed awake for 33.5 hours because he was bouncing around on a hard board. The silly guy had almost no sleep for a whole day before he even took off. The hindrance of restlessness and worry kept him awake, thinking about his flight.

The simile for dullness and drowsiness is of a pot of slimy water with water plants growing on top so you can't see your reflection.

4. Restlessness and Remorse

Restlessness is the agitated state of mind when you can't settle down and focus on anything or pay attention to what you are doing or what people are saying to you. This forth hindrance includes worry, regret and guilt, thoughts that keep coming back to pray on you, unless they are another hindrance. It can be caused by the fault-finding mind which is dissatisfied with things as they are. It's looking for something better, forever just beyond. Buddha compared restlessness to being a slave, always having to jump to the orders of a domineering boss who demands perfection and never lets one stop. Contentment can overcome this because it's the opposite of fault finding. Learn to be satisfied with what you have instead of always wanting more. Be happy, relax and shut up that churning mind.

When you get restless in meditation that means that you're still holding onto something, you're pushing or pulling so just let go... of the mind until the restless thoughts fade out into a background hum. Get an aerial view of your mind and watch the thoughts and feelings flow. Be more in your awareness, observing the thoughts go by. A restless cow is released from a pen so she runs and runs across a field and she eats and eats until finally she just sits down comfortably because her restlessness becomes irrelevant. Repeating a mantra is a basic way to knock out restless thoughts by replacing them with the word or phrase you are repeating to yourself.

Nyanaponika writes (B.P.S., 1993; 22):

> Six things are conducive to the abandonment of restlessness and remorse:
> 1. Knowledge of the Buddhist scriptures (Doctrine and Discipline);
> 2. Asking questions about them;
> 3. Familiarity with the Vinaya (the Code of Monastic Discipline, and for lay followers, with the principles of moral conduct);
> 4. Association with those mature in age and experience, who possess dignity, restraint and calm;
> 5. Noble friendship;
> 6. Suitable conversation.

These things, too, are helpful in conquering restlessness and remorse:

- Rapture, of the factors of absorption (jhananga);
- Concentration, of the spiritual faculties (indriya);
- Tranquility, concentration and equanimity, of the factors of enlightenment (bojjhanga).

Indriya means spiritual faculties. Wikipedia describes indriya:

SN 48.10 is one of several discourses that characterizes these spiritual faculties in the following manner:

- **Faith/Conviction** is faith in the Buddha's *awakening*.
- **Energy/Persistence** refers to exertion towards the *Four Right Efforts*.
- **Mindfulness** refers to focusing on the four *satipatthana*.
- **Concentration** refers to achieving the four *jhanas*.
- **Wisdom/Understanding** refers to discerning the *Four Noble Truths*.

In SN 48.51, the Buddha declares that, of these five faculties, wisdom is the "chief" (*agga*).

The first three in the list above, about eliminating restlessness, point out the foundation of the the Buddhist path which is sila, or virtue. If you follow the precepts well then you will have more peace. It is unwholesome actions of body, speech or mind that result in worry, restlessness and remorse. So it is good to study what the dhamma means by virtue; have a thorough understanding of what virtuous behaviour is, beginning with the five precepts. Remorse and regret come from doing things we wished we hadn't or not doing things we wished we had. Guilt comes with that but it is best to let go of guilt and leave the past in the past. If you have done something wrong it is wise to recognize that and resolve not to do it again, but to hang on to regret and feeling guilty is a negative thought pattern. A negative thought pattern will only cause you to make even more unskilful actions in the future so just leave the past in the past. Let it go.

From the view of karma there's no need to feel guilty because your negative karma will probably catch up to you anyway! Feeling guilty isn't going to erase it so you might as well just lighten up with a smile. Ajahn Brahm says ("Five Hindrances," 1999):

> Remorse refers to a specific type of restlessness which is the kammic effect of one's misdeeds. The only way to overcome remorse, the restlessness of a bad conscience, is to purify one's virtue and become kind, wise and gentle. It is virtually impossible for the immoral or the self indulgent to make deep progress in meditation.

Ajahn Sucitto in England teaches "Worry more deliberately and slowly and peacefully. This throws it out of sync. Or worry more quickly or set a time for worry. You're taking away the compulsive quality of it; you're adjusting it." You could decide to worry about your problem only between 5:00 – 6:00 pm. That way you feel that you're not ignoring it; you're still attending to it. And then think about the situation at that time. If you don't feel like doing it, then you're getting over it. To reduce worry you can take a freeze frame picture in your mind of what you're worrying about. Changing the speed breaks up the obsessive quality of worry because you can't keep worrying like that. It helps to break it up.

The Buddha again,:

> When the mind is restless it is not the proper time for cultivating the following factors of enlightenment: investigation of the doctrine, energy and rapture, because an agitated mind can hardly be quietened by them.

> When the mind is restless, it is the proper time for cultivating the following factors of enlightenment: tranquility, concentration and equanimity, because an agitated mind can easily be quietened by them." — SN 46:53

The simile for restless and worry is of a pot of water that has wind blowing on the surface making ripples so you can't see your reflection.

5. *Doubt*

The last hindrance of doubt is a problematic wavering, indecision, an inability to make up your mind and commit yourself to something. This can be doubt about the Buddha's teachings or self doubt. A hindrance means that if you have already tested the Buddhist teachings on meditation and you have had good results, then doubt could just be from discouragement or inner turmoil, not related to a justifiable doubt. It's good to have a discerning mind and probe into things and be circumspect. The Buddha told the Kalamas that it is wise to have doubt in a matter which is doubtful. It's OK to doubt. The Buddha said come and see, not come and believe. That's not a hindrance, that's intelligence. What we're talking about here is a mental hindrance where you backslide into unwholesome thoughts like, "I can't meditate because I think too much." "This isn't right for me." As it relates to our self doubt, when we are in a clear, happy state of mind and we see the rightness in practicing our good habits and vanquishing our bad habits, we should write that down for ourselves and remember to read it later when we are beset by doubt, uncertainty and temptation. Human beings forget! We forget the most important things sometimes so you should become a fundamentalist of your own writings and stick to that.

Lord Buddha compared doubt to being in a caravan with valuable goods, crossing a dessert, lost, worried about thieves. When you have made it to a town safely, you are relieved. Doubt is dispelled. You want to restore confidence. You can interrogate the doubt and gather clear instructions, like having a good map. Nurture confidence by having a good teacher. A meditation teacher is like a spiritual coach who encourages you and convinces you that you can succeed. Of the antidotes to doubt, the first three and the last two are identical with those given for restlessness and remorse above. The fourth is as follows: Firm conviction concerning the Buddha, Dhamma and Sangha. The simile for doubt is that it is like a bowl of muddy water put in a dark place, so you can't see your reflection.

In conclusion, so long as these five hindrances are not abandoned in you, you can consider yourself as indebted, as ailing, as imprisoned, as enslaved and as traveling in a wilderness. You can find your way through the hindrances one day, then they come back. You can have insight but lose it. The path keeps bringing you back if you keep practicing dhamma. The text of the Discourse says: "But when these five hindrances are abandoned, the monk considers himself as free from debt, rid of illness, emancipated from the prison's bondage, as a free man, and as one arrived at a place of safety." Even with all of your existing hindrances right now, you can focus the mind on the below exercise to determine your direction in life. I'll complete the book on that note.

Meaning and Purpose in Life

The search for meaning and purpose in life is your meaning and purpose in life. This should be your aspiration until you decide what your major definite purpose is. A Buddhist can plug into the Buddhist meaning of life, as outlined in the noble eightfold path, but for people who are not Buddhists, we will explore the process and the questions through which you can determine what your place is in the big picture, and how you should best proceed. Looking back over the lives of great people, all of the lives that became great did so after the selection of a major definite purpose. People say, "Well, I finally decided to get serious, and . . ." the rest is history. Prince Siddhartha decided to find a solution to death itself. You can have clearly written and defined goals with regard to many things but you must have one, just one major goal in life. Carl Jung, the Swiss psychologist said, "I made it my task of tasks in life to find a mythology by which to live." That was his major purpose in life. What is yours? You must select one in order for your subconscious mind to take you seriously and help you significantly, because lots of people just have ideas but few act. You must be strong in the power of your inner convictions.

There is a set of seven questions below which you should only give yourself one minute per question to answer. Get out a pen and clean sheet of paper and write down the answers. It is recommended that you read a good dharma book several times because then you get more and more at deeper levels of mind. Each time, do these seven questions again, and see how the answers change, or stay the same. After you have read this book and answered these questions a second time, you will know that the time has arrived for you to select your major definite purpose in life. Here are the seven questions:

1. What five things do you value most in life? Sex? Lots of money? Material possessions? Your spiritual path? The love of your family and friends? Your political beliefs? Your computer and the Internet? What five things? Afterwards, organize them in order of priority.

2. What would you do if you had only six months left to live? Whatever it is, you should be doing it now because we never know when we only have six months to live. Who would you call? What would you do with your money and your will? What projects would you complete or initiate? Who would you spend your time with?

3. What would you do if you suddenly inherited $20,000,000? What would you do if you had all the time and money in the world? Would you stay in the relationship you are in? Would you quit your job? If so, then maybe you should quit your job soon, because it is the wrong job for you and you are wasting your time, and wasting your life. What would you do if you were free to choose?

4. What one thing would you do if you knew that you could not fail? If you had only one magic pill, what would you ask the devas for if you knew that once you swallowed the pill, you would absolutely for sure get just that one thing? What would it be? What one great thing would you dare to do if you knew you could not fail? Would you run for public office? Whatever it is, you can achieve it if you are willing to pay the price.

5. What are your three most important goals in life right now? This indicates the three most important concerns that you have right now.
6. What have you always wanted to do but have been afraid to attempt? This answer reveals the ego's self limiting belief or block that is holding you back.
7. What activities in your life have given you the greatest feeling of importance and self esteem? When have you been the happiest in life? What were you doing? This answer leads you unerringly to your true area of excellence. Past life talents may have been in that area.

Remember, only give yourself one minute to answer each of these seven questions. If you gave yourself two hours, your answer would probably be less honest than with one minute. The reason for this is because you would have too much time to second guess your heartfelt response, and you would rationalize and change it around so it would seem to appear right. So, be totally open and honest with yourself. No one else needs to read this.

The author with two Thai monks at Wat Ram Poeng

A Short Walk On An Ancient Path

Bibliography

Publications

Bodhi, Bhikkhu. *The Noble Eightfold Path: The Way to the End of Suffering.* Kandy: B.P.S., 1994.

Bodhi, Bhikkhu. "Climbing to the Top of the Mountain." *Insight Journal* 19 (2002) n. pag.

Brahm, Ajahn. *Mindfulness, Bliss, and Beyond – A Meditator's Handbook.* Boston: Wisdom Publications, 2006.

Buddhaghosa, *Acariya. Path of Purification.* Trans. Bhikkhu Nanamoli. Singapore Meditation Centre, 1956.

Chah, Ajahn. *No Ajahn Chah – Reflections.* Taiwan: Dhamma Garden, 1994.

Connected Discourses of the Buddha (Samyutta Nikaya). Trans. Bhikkhu Bodhi. Boston: Wisdom Publications, 2000.

Dhammananda, Ven. Dr. K. "The Significance of the Transference of Merits to the Departed." Web. 1987.

Joyce, James. *Ulysses.* London: Penguin, 2000 (original 1922).

Kusalo, Ajahn. "Walking Meditation." Web. n.d. Ottawa: BuddhaMind.info

Lama, Dalai. *A Policy of Kindness.* Ithaca: Snow Lion Publications, 1990.

The Long Discourses of the Buddha (Digha Nikaya). Trans. by Maurice Walshe. London: Wisdom Publications, 1987.

The Middle Length Discourses of the Buddha – A New Translation of the Majjhima Nikaya. Trans. Nanamoli Bhikkhu, and Bhikkhu Bodhi. Boston: Wisdom Publications, 1995.

Numbered Discourses – Book of the Threes. Tipitaka: The Pali Canon, by John T. Bullitt. Access to Insight, 2009, accesstoinsight.org.

Thera, Nyanaponika. *The Five Mental Hindrances and Their Conquest.* Kandy: B.P.S., 1993.

Mahathera, Nyanatiloka. *The Word of the Buddha.* 17th edition. Kandy: Buddhist Publication Society, 2001.

The Questions of King Milinda. Trans. T.W. Rhys Davids. Whitefish, MT: Kessinger, 2004.

Rahula, Walpola. *What the Buddha Taught.* Taipei: Corporate Body, Buddha Educational Foundation, 1959.

Ramster, Peter. *The Search for Lives Past.* Brisbane: Somerset, 1992.

Silananda, U. *Paritta Pali and Protective Suttas.* Penang: Inward Path, 1995.

Sona, Ajahn. "Meditation on Breathing, Meditation on Loving Kindness." 2001. Web. birken.ca.

Stevenson, Dr. Ian. *Xenoglossy: A Review and Report of a Case.* Charlottesville: U. of Virginia Press, 1974.

Stevenson, Dr. Ian. *Where Reincarnation and Biology Intersect.* Westport CT: Praeger, 1997.

Sucitto, Ajahn. *Kalyana – Dhamma Talks from Ajahn Sucitto.* 2nd ed. revised. Amaravati Publications, 2002.

Bhikkhu, Thanissaro. *Wings to Awakening: An Anthology from the Pali Canon.* 3rd ed. revised. Barre: Dhamma Dana, 1999.

Trungpa, Chögyam. *Heart of the Buddha.* Boston: Shambhala, 1991.

Audiocassettes

Bodhi, Bhikkhu. *The Buddha's Teaching As It Is.* Kandy: B.P.S., 1984.

Sona, Ajahn. *Kamma and Rebirth.* Birken Forest Monastery, 2003.

Tracy, Brian. *The Phoenix Seminar. Peak Performance Training/ Brian Tracy,* 1987.

Tendzin, Vajra Regent Osel. *Discipline.* Halifax: Kalapa Recordings, 1988.

Television Programs

Sagan, Carl. *Cosmos.* Carl Sagan Productions. PBS. 1980.

Thai maechees ringing gongs

Burmese monks at a shrine

Recommended Reading

(Sitavana) Birken Forest Monastery Recommended Book List

[Abbreviation: BPS = Buddhist Publication Society]

Beginners

Meditation

Mindfulness in Plain English, by Ven. Gunaratana (Wisdom)

Calm and Insight: A Buddhist Manual for Meditators, by Bhikkhu Khantipalo (Curzon)

Buddhist Teachings and Practice

The Power of Mindfulness, by Nyanaponika Thera (BPS).

The Word of the Buddha, by Nyanatiloka Thera (BPS).

Going for Refuge: Taking the Precepts, by Bhikkhu Bodhi (BPS).

The Noble Eightfold Path, by Bhikkhu Bodhi (BPS).

The Buddha and His Teachings, by Narada Mahathera (BPS).

Metta: The Philosophy and Practice of Universal Love, by Acariya Buddharakkhita (BPS).

Loving-Kindness: The Revolutionary Art of Happiness, by Sharon Salzberg (Shambhala).

Mudita: The Buddha's Teaching on Unselfish Joy, ed. by Nyanaponika Thera (BPS).

Dana: The Practice of Giving, ed. by Bhikkhu Bodhi (BPS).

Kamma and Its Fruit, by Nyanaponika Thera (BPS).

Who Ordered this Truckload of Dung? Inspiring Stories for Welcoming Life's Difficulties, by Ajahn Brahm (Wisdom).

The Questions of King Milinda (Milindapanha), trans. by N. Mendis (BPS).

Suttas

Everyman's Ethics, Narada Mahathera (BPS).

The Scale of Good Deeds, Susan Elbaum Jootla (BPS).

The Buddha's Teaching in His Own Words, Bhikkhu Nanamoli (BPS).

Intermediate & Advanced

Meditation

The Heart of Buddhist Meditation, by Nyanaponika Thera (BPS).

Mindfulness, Bliss, and Beyond, by Ajahn Brahm (Wisdom)

Mindfulness in Plain English, by Ven. Henepola Gunaratana (Wisdom).

Satipatthana: The Direct Path to Realization, by Analayo (Windhorse).

The Four Foundations of Mindfulness, by Ven. U Silananda (Wisdom).

The Jhanas (in Theravada Buddhist Meditation), by Ven. Henepola Gunaratana (BPS).

The Path of Serenity and Insight, by Bhante Henepola Gunaratana (Motilal Banarsidass).

The Seven Contemplations of Insight: A Treatise on Insight Meditation, by Ven. Matara Sri Nanarama Mahathera (BPS).

In This Very Life: Liberations Teachings of the Buddha, by Sayadaw U Pandita (Wisdom).

Who is My Self? A Guide to Buddhist Meditation, by Ayya Khema (Wisdom).

Buddhist Teachings and Practice

In the Buddha's Words: An Anthology of Discourses from the Pali Canon, trans. and intro. by Bhikkhu Bodhi (Wisdom)

The Noble Eightfold Path, by Bhikkhu Bodhi (BPS).

Eight Mindful Steps to Happiness, by Bhante Henepola Gunaratana (Wisdom).

The Vision of Dhamma, by Nyanaponika Thera (BPS) [also from Rider].

Path to Deliverance, by Nyanatiloka Thera (BPS).

The Road to Inner Freedom, ed. by Nyanaponika Thera (BPS).

What the Buddha Taught, by Walpola Rahula (Grove Weidenfeld).

The Buddha and His Teachings, by Narada Thera (BPS).

The Buddha's Ancient Path, by Piyadassi Thera (BPS).

Food for the Heart: The Collected Teachings of Ajahn Chah, by Ajahn Chah (Wisdom)

Everything Arises, Everything Falls Away: Teachings on Impermanence and the End of Suffering, by Ajahn Chah (Shambhala).

Being Dharma:The Essence of the Buddha's Teachings, by Ajahn Chah (Shambhala).

A Still Forest Pool: The Insight Meditation of Achaan Chah, ed. by Jack Kornfield + Paul Breiter (Quest); [also available from BPS]

Being Nobody, Going Nowhere, by Ayya Khema (Wisdom).

Be an Island: The Buddhist Practice of Inner Peace, by Ayya Khema (Wisdom).

When the Iron Eagle Flies: Buddhism for the West, by Ayya Khema (Wisdom).

Questions From the City -Answers From the Forest, by Ajahn Sumano Bhikkhu (Quest).

Landscapes of Wonder, by Bhikkhu Nyanasobhano (Wisdom).

The Word of the Buddha, by Nyanatiloka Thera (BPS).

The Life of the Buddha According to the Pali Canon, by Bhikkhu Namamoli (BPS).

Great Disciples of the Buddha, ed. by Nyanaponika Thera, Hellmuth Hecker + Bhikkhu Bodhi (BP); [also available from Wisdom].

The Wings to Awakening, by Thanissaro Bhikkhu (for free distribution - Dhamma Dana Publications, Barre Center for Buddhist Studies).

Buddhadhamma: Natural Laws and Values for Life, by Phra Prayudh Payutto (State University of New York Press).

Pali Canon & Commentaries

The Long Discourses of the Buddha (Digha Nikaya), trans. by Maurice Walshe (Wisdom); [also available from BPS].

The Middle Length Discourses of the Buddha (Majjhima Nikaya), trans. by Bhikkhu Nanamoli + Bhikkhu Bodhi (Wisdom); [also available from BPS].

The Connected Discourses of the Buddha (Samyutta Nikaya), 2 vols., trans. by Bhikkhu Bodhi (Wisdom).

Numerical Discourses of the Buddha (Anthology of Anguttara Nikaya), trans. by Nyanaponika Thera + Bhikkhu Bodhi (Altamira Press).

The Itivuttaka: The Buddha's Sayings, trans. by John D. Ireland (BPS).

The Udana: Inspired Utterances of the Buddha, trans. by John D. Ireland (BPS).

The Path of Discrimination (Patisambhidamagga), trans. by Bhikkhu Nanamoli (Pali Text Society).

The Path of Freedom (Vimuttimagga), trans. by Rev. N.R.M. Ehara, Soma Thera + Kheminda Thera (BPS).

The Path of Purification (Visuddhimagga), Buddhaghosa, trans. by Bhikkhu Nanamoli (BPS).

A Comprehensive Manual of Abhidhamma (Abhidhammattha Sanghaha), ed. by Bhikkhu Bodhi (BPS).

Reference

Buddhist Dictionary: Manual of Terms and Doctrines, by Nyanatiloka Thera (BPS).

Rebirth as Doctrine and Experience, by Francis Story (BPS).

Twenty Cases Suggestive of Reincarnation, by Ian Stevenson, M.D. (University Press of Virginia).

Where Reincarnation and Biology Intersect, by Ian Stevenson, M.D. (Praeger Publishers).

Buddhist Monastic Life, by Mohan Wijayaratna (Cambridge University Press).

Some Valuable Online Sources of Buddhist texts available by donation, or as PDFs:

Access to Insight

Abhayagiri Buddhist Monastery

Amaravati Buddhist Monastery

Aruna Ratanagiri Buddhist Monastery

Buddhist Publication Society

Online, Free Buddhist Texts:

The Basic Method of Meditation, by Ajahn Brahmavamso

Mindfulness in Plain English, by Ven. Gunaratana

The Teachings of Ajahn Chah: A Collection of Ajahn Chah's Translated Dhamma Talks, compiled by the Sangha at Wat Pah Nanachat

The Wings to Awakening: An Anthology from the Pali Canon, by Thanissaro Bhikkhu

Ayuthaya – Wat Phra Sri Samphet

Glossary

abhidhamma

> Third basket of scriptures, a technical and very detailed analysis of the mind and the universe.

arahant

> A fully enlightened person.

ascetic

> One who leads a very austere and self-denying life, a yogi, Prince Siddhartha before his discovery of the middle way.

asura

> A jealous god deva, titan, demon.

bhavana

> Mental development or culture, meditation. lit. "calling into existence, producing."

blessing

> The transformation of our mind from the inspiration of our spiritual guide or devas.

bodhi

> Awake, awakenment, enlightenment. From verbal root budhi, to awaken, to understand.

bodhisatta

> "Enlightenment Being," is a being destined to Buddhahood, a future Buddha. In the Theravada Pali Canon, this designation is given only to Prince Siddhartha before his enlightenment and to his former existences (Nyanatiloka, 1980; 41). There is only one at a time per world system. While Metteya is mentioned in the Pali Canon he is not referred to as a bodhisatta, but simply the next fully-awakened Buddha to come into existence long after the current teachings of the Buddha are lost.

Brahma

> The greatest of the brahmas in the cosmos, the Hindu God; also meaning "the highest."

Brahma Viharas
Four "divine abodes," the contemplations on loving kindness, compassion, altruistic joy, equanimity.

Brahmin
The highest caste in Indian society, the religious leaders.

Buddha
self awakened man, Siddhartha Gotama.

dana
Generosity, giving, offering, particularly to the Buddhist sangha.

deva
Heavenly beings in the god realm, angels

dhamma or dharma
The Buddhist teachings, natural law, the way things are.

dukkha
The first noble truth of suffering, impermanence, insubstantiality, etc.

ego
Self, belief in the existence of a self.

emptiness
Empty of the nature of a separate independent self.

enlightenment
The ultimate goal of the Buddhist religion, the final extinction of suffering, nirvana, a state of mind impossible to define.

hindrances
sensual desire, anger, dullness and drowsiness, worry and restlessness, doubt

jhana
meditation absorption state of one-pointed concentration with all five senses absent. Eight levels.

kalpa

An age, varying in length, approximately an ice age, subdivided into four sections.

karma

Volitional actions, or intentional actions, not the results of karma.

kasina

An external meditation object used to develop concentration.

kilesa

defilements or corruptions, passion, aggression and ignorance

loka

"World," the whole universe.

lokapala

The deva/s associated with a particular geographic location.

mantra

"That which the mind leans against," or "mind protection." A word or phrase repeated by oneself as a meditation object.

merit

Good karma created by virtuous actions.

mindfulness

Keeping your mind on what you are doing while you are doing it, not straying from the present. Keeping something in mind. Remembering the instructions. Remembering to stay present.

nirvana

Enlightenment.

paramis

the ten perfections. Generosity (dana). Virtue (sila). Renunciation (nekkhamma). Wisdom (panna). Energy (viriya). Patience (khanti). Truthfulness (sacca). Determination (aditthana). Loving kindness (metta). Equanimity (upekkha).

panna

Insight, discriminating awareness, wisdom.

peta

Ghost.

realms

The five realms of existence where all beings live: human, devas and asuras, animal, ghost, hell.

rebirth

Reunion, relinking, of the five aggregates after death into any one of the realms. Human rebirth arises around the time of conception with the forming of new life in the mother's womb.

refuge

Committing oneself to the Buddha, dharma and sangha as your spiritual guide.

Sakka

"King of the gods," principal deva and lord over Tavatimsa heaven, second heaven in the sensuous sphere.

samadhi

A state of sustained concentration on a meditation object, mental focus or composing the mind.

samsara

The world of suffering, continuous struggle, "round of rebirth," lit. "perpetual wandering."

sangha

Buddhist community of saints. Wider meaning: four or more monastics; or just a meditation group.

sasana

(lit. "message"): the Dispensation of the Buddha, the Buddhist religion; teaching, doctrine — it's time period on earth.

sentient being

A being of limited awareness.

sila

Morality, discipline.

kandhas or aggregates

Five parts of the self: form, feeling, perception, mental formations and consciousness.

sutta

"From the mouth of the Buddha," a discourse of the Buddha, the suttas.

Tathagata

"Perfect One," "thus gone," an epithet of the Buddha referring to himself.

Theravada

"Doctrine of the elders" the southern school of Buddhism, closest to the original teachings of the Buddha.

Tripitaka

"Three baskets" of the canonical Theravada Buddhist scriptures: suttas, vinaya and abhidhamma.

Vinaya

The second basket of original scriptures in the tripitaka, the moral rules of conduct for monks and nuns, and laymen also.

Vipassana

Insight, wisdom, that is the decisive liberating factor in Buddhism, the intuitive light flashing forth and exposing the truth of impermanency, the suffering and the impersonal and insubstantial nature of all corporeal and mental phenomena of existence (Nyanatiloka, 1980; 230).

wheel

a wheel with eight spokes represents the Buddha's eightfold path to enlightenment. Theravada Buddhist symbol, as well as the most universal symbol of the Buddhist religion. Sometimes depicted with a thousand spokes.

Statue of a wandering forest monk in Thailand

About the Author

Brian Anthony Ruhe, born Dec. 31, 1959, trained as a monk in Thailand and has taught Buddhism since 1996 in the Vancouver, BC area. He has taught thousands of people at temples, community colleges, the University of the Fraser Valley, and at adult education courses in school boards and community centres.

Raised within a Unitarian background, Brian was exposed early to the spiritual dimension of life. Originally from Ontario, he studied business and philosophy at Brock University, and moved to Vancouver in 1980. After completing his studies at BCIT he worked in the financial planning industry for eight years. Although he was a reasonably happy individual, he felt that something was 'missing' from his life. Like many of us, he was haunted by the need for meaning and purpose in life.

Brian considered a number of spiritual paths. In 1991 he was drawn to Buddhism which he found to be sane, profound and wise. After immersing himself in Buddhist teachings he left the financial planning business, and became a true seeker. The first stage of his journey was a six-month stay at a Tibetan Buddhist centre in Vermont, founded by Chogyam Trungpa, after which he moved for four years to Thailand, a Theravada Buddhist country. In Thailand he studied and practised at various temples and meditation centres, gathering teachings and deepening his meditation practice. He was ordained and spent a short time in the robes with the name Buddhasaro Bhikkhu (see photo next page). At his home temple, Wat Ram Poeng, in Chiangmai, Northern Thailand, he was trained by the abbot, Ajahn Supan, to be a Vipassana meditation instructor. It was here that Brian first began to teach and give formal lectures on Buddhism to the dozens of Westerners who came to the monastery for month-long meditation retreats. It was in this setting that Brian decided it was time to return to Canada to share his insights and experiences. He has founded meditation groups and is now a student of Ajahn Sona in the Theravada Forest tradition of Ajahn Chah. Ajahn Sona is abbot of the Birken Forest Monastery near Kamloops, BC. Ajahn Sona's wisdom, knowledge and sense of humour have been a guiding inspiration for Brian since they met in 2000.

Brian Ruhe when he was a monk in Thailand, 1996

To Contact Brian Ruhe:
Website: www.theravada.ca
Email: brian@theravada.ca
Telephone: (604) 738-8475
Home address:
#104 - 1960 West 7th Ave., Vancouver, BC V6J 1T1

(Sitavana) Birken Forest Monastery (www.birken.ca)
Contains thousands of free dhamma talks for downloading.

A Short Walk On An Ancient Path